CHARLES DE FOUCAULD

MODERN SPIRITUAL MASTERS
Robert Ellsberg, Series Editor

This series introduces the writing and vision of some of the great spiritual masters of the twentieth century. Along with selections from their writings, each volume includes a comprehensive introduction, presenting the author's life and writings in context and drawing attention to points of special relevance to contemporary spirituality.

Some of these authors found a wide audience in their lifetimes. In other cases recognition has come long after their deaths. Some are rooted in long-established traditions of spirituality. Others charted new, untested paths. In each case, however, the authors in this series have engaged in a spiritual journey shaped by the influences and concerns of our age. Such concerns include the challenges of modern science, religious pluralism, secularism, and the quest for social justice.

At the dawn of a new millennium this series commends these modern spiritual masters, along with the saints and witnesses of previous centuries, as guides and companions to a new generation of seekers.

Already published:
Dietrich Bonhoeffer (edited by Robert Coles)
Simone Weil (edited by Eric O. Springsted)
Henri Nouwen (edited by Robert A. Jonas)

Forthcoming volumes include:
Pierre Teilhard de Chardin (edited by Ursula King)
Karl Rahner
Oscar Romero
John Main
Flannery O'Connor
Brother Roger of Taizé

CHARLES DE FOUCAULD

*Writings Selected
with an Introduction by*

ROBERT ELLSBERG

ORBIS BOOKS

Maryknoll, New York 10545

The Catholic Foreign Mission Society of America (Maryknoll) recruits and trains people for overseas missionary service. Through Orbis Books, Maryknoll aims to foster the international dialogue that is essential to mission. The books published, however, reflect the opinions of their authors and are not meant to represent the official position of the society.

Copyright © 1999 by Orbis Books

Introduction copyright © 1996, 1999 by Robert Ellsberg
An earlier version of the introduction was published in Susan Bergman, ed., *Martyrs: Contemporary Writers on Modern Lives of Faith* (San Francisco: HarperCollins, 1996; Maryknoll, NY: Orbis Books, 1998).

Published by Orbis Books, Maryknoll, NY 10545-0308

Manufactured in the United States of America

Library of Congress Cataloging-in-Publication Data
Foucauld, Charles de, 1858–1916.
   [Selections. 1999]
   Charles de Foucauld : writings / selected with an introduction by
Robert Ellsberg.
      p. cm. – (Modern spiritual masters series)
   Includes bibliographical references.
   ISBN 1-57075-244-3 (pbk.)
   1. Foucauld, Charles de, 1858–1916. 2. Spiritual life – Catholic
Church. I. Ellsberg, Robert, 1955– . II. Title. III. Series.
BX4705.F65A25 1999
282 – dc21
                                                         98-31860

Contents

Sources

CG   *Cry the Gospel with Your Life* by the Little Brothers and Little Sisters of Jesus (Denville, N.J.: Dimension Books, 1981).

Carrouges   *Soldier of the Spirit: The Life of Charles de Foucauld* by Michel Carrouges, trans. Marie-Christine Hellin (New York: G. P. Putnam's Sons, 1956).

Faith   *Scriptural Meditations on Faith* by Charles de Foucauld, trans. Alexandra Russell (New York: New City Press, 1988).

Hope   *Hope in the Gospels* by Charles de Foucauld, trans. Nelly Marans (New York: New City Press, 1990).

Memories   *Memories of Charles de Foucauld, Explorer and Hermit: Seen in His Letters* by Father George Gorrée, trans. Donald Attwater (London: Burns Oates & Washbourne, 1938).

MH   *Meditations of a Hermit* by Charles de Foucauld, trans. Charlotte Balfour (London: Burns and Oates, and Maryknoll, N.Y.: Orbis Books, 1981).

SA   *Spiritual Autobiography of Charles de Foucauld,* ed. Jean-François Six, trans. H. Holland Smith (New York: P. J. Kenedy & Sons, 1964).

Sermons   *Sermons in the Sahara: A Simple Introduction to the Christian Gospel* by Charles de Foucauld, trans. Donald Attwater (London: Burns Oates & Washbourne, 1938).

SP   *Silent Pilgrimage to God: The Spirituality of Charles de Foucauld* by A Little Brother of Jesus, trans. Jeremy Moiser (London: Darton, Longman and Todd, and Maryknoll, N.Y.: Orbis Books, 1974).

Witness   *Witness in the Desert: The Life of Charles de Foucauld* by Jean-François Six, trans. Lucie Noel (New York: Macmillan, 1965). Copyright © 1962 by Editions du Seuil. (Reprinted by permission of Georges Borchardt, Inc.)

Grateful acknowledgment is made to the above-cited publishers for permission to reprint copyrighted materials.

Preface

I no longer want a monastery which is too secure. I want a small monastery, like the house of a poor work-man who is not sure if tomorrow he will find work and bread, who with all his being shares the suffering of the world.

By any conventional standard, the life of Charles de Foucauld (1858–1916) — soldier, explorer, monk, and ultimately desert hermit — ended in failure. At the time of his violent death he had published none of his spiritual writings; he had founded no congregation nor had he attracted any followers. He could not even claim responsibility for a single conversion. And yet, in time, many would regard him as one of the great spiritual figures of the twentieth century. The credit for this posthumous appeal owed little to Foucauld's scattered writings. More important was the power of his spiritual vision, embodied in a life of singular purpose. Foucauld was one of those seekers who, periodically, manage to reinvent the "imitation of Christ" in a manner suited to the needs of their age, and thus invite others to read the Gospel in a new way.

· Among his achievements, Foucauld was largely responsible for rediscovering the wisdom of the ancient desert fathers. Without rejecting the value of communal monasticism, he believed that time spent alone with God enables us truly to know and love our neighbors as ourselves. He was equally influential in his approach to mission. In contrast

to the triumphalistic models of his day, Foucauld exempli-
fied an evangelism of presence, a willingness to encounter
people of other faiths on a basis of equality and mutual respect. Furthermore, he pioneered a new model of religious
life, patterned after the life of Jesus himself, whose only clois-
ter was the world of the poor. In a century exhausted by
grand projects, world wars, and ostentatious display, Foucauld's appreciation for the value of inconspicuous means,
modest goals, and the hidden life of faith and charity exerts
a powerful and subversive challenge. It reminds us, among
other things, that Christ himself pursued the path of appar-
ent failure, choosing "what is low and despised in the world,
even things that are not, to bring to nothing things that are"
(1 Cor. 1:28).

Twenty years after Foucauld's lonely death his spiritual vision was taken up by René Voillaume and Madeleine Hutin,
founders respectively of the Little Brothers and the Little Sisters of Jesus. Through these congregations and their several
offshoots the spirit of Foucauld has spread to the far corners
of the globe, aided by the writings of such figures as Arturo
Paoli, Carlo Carretto, and Voillaume himself. Foucauld's
own writings, in the meantime, have remained relatively obscure — at least to an English-speaking audience. Though
published in many volumes in France, relatively little of Foucauld's work has appeared in English. None of the sources
for this selection is currently in print.

Foucauld, in any case, never envisioned a literary legacy.
Though an avid correspondent and a somewhat less consistent journal writer, he did not generally write for an audience
wider than himself and one or two others. He kept note-
books during his regular retreats, returning again and again
to a fairly consistent range of his favorite themes. But it
is clear that the overriding stress in his writings is not on

his own originality, but on the life of Jesus, the pattern for all Christian discipleship and spirituality. Nevertheless, Foucauld's writings bear the vivid stamp of his personality and a holy wisdom forged in the light of his desert vigil. The present selection affords an opportunity for his distinctive vision to shine forth to a new generation.

I first encountered the legacy of Charles de Foucauld many years ago through a fraternity of Little Brothers of the Gospel, who lived on the Lower East Side of Manhattan. By day they worked in menial jobs, as janitors, hospital orderlies, or factory workers. But the center of their lives was the friendship and community they shared with their poor neighbors. At the heart of it all was the beautifully decorated chapel in their tenement apartment, an oasis of love in the midst of the urban desert. It was there, where the Little Brothers gathered each evening for silent adoration, that I first comprehended the meaning of the Real Presence.

To the Little Brothers of that fraternity of long ago — Giorgio, Maurice, Jay, Pat — and to Father Peter Raphael, this volume is gratefully dedicated.

Little Brother of Jesus

On the evening of December 1, 1916, Charles de Foucauld was roused from his prayers by an urgent knock on the door of his hermitage in Tamanrasset, a remote outpost in the Saharan desert of Algeria. Foucauld, the only Catholic priest within many hundreds of miles, was known as the *Marabout,* or holy man. It was a mark of respect on the part of his Tuareg neighbors. Devout Muslims, they respected the Frenchman's piety and good works, though they were not tempted to share his faith.

Despite the isolation of his hermitage, Brother Charles was accustomed to receiving visitors at all hours. Part of his mission as a "little brother of Jesus" was to remain available to the needs of his neighbors. But lately he had taken unusual precautions. The reverberations of the Great War in Europe were felt even in this isolated corner of the desert. He had been warned that Tuareg rebels, inspired by a brotherhood of Muslim fanatics, might be looking for an opportunity to strike a blow against the French infidels. Thus he had lately fortified his hermitage, and he did not answer a knock at the door without determining the identity of his caller.

The desert sand had muffled the sound of camels and the dismounting of the forty armed men who now surrounded his little fort. The caller identified himself as the mailman. In fact he was a local tribesman, known to Charles, who had accepted a bribe to transact this betrayal. Trustingly, Charles unbolted the door and reached out his hand, only to be roughly seized. The rebels poured in and bound his arms. While some subjected him to interrogation others searched the hermitage for valuables. Charles did not answer their questions, but only seemed to pray silently while a fifteen-year-old boy pressed a rifle against his temple. When twenty minutes had elapsed a noise was heard, the sound of two approaching camels. Charles started to move, whereupon his frightened guard shot the priest through the head.

Foucauld's lonely death was in character with the solitude and obscurity of his life. He had spent years in the desert preparing the way for followers who never arrived, and his efforts had ended this way, with a shot in the dark, a sound quickly absorbed in the cold sand of the surrounding dunes. Compared to the rivers of blood then flowing through Europe, it was a relatively unremarkable event. No one could have anticipated the extent of his later influence, the fact that several congregations would trace their foundation to his inspiration, that indeed Charles de Foucauld would come to be regarded as one of the most significant religious figures of the twentieth century. But in fact the path between his death and his later influence is far less remarkable than the path that led to his final appointment in Tamanrasset.

Viscount Charles-Eugène de Foucauld was born in Strasbourg on September 15, 1858, to a proudly aristocratic family. Throughout his childhood he was regaled with stories of his ancestors' honor and of their history of service to cross and crown. The Foucaulds, he learned, had fought in the Crusades and stood beside Joan of Arc at Orleans, thus earning the family a title and a coat of arms emblazoned with a heroic motto: *Never Retreat*. Of the varieties of valor, however, his pious mother paid special tribute to the example of Armand de Foucauld, archbishop of Arles, who had died a martyr during the revolutionary terror of 1792. But Charles's mother was given little time to impart her faith and ideals. She died in childbirth when Charles was six, a loss compounded only six months later by his father's death from tuberculosis.

Charles and his younger sister were entrusted to their maternal grandfather, a retired colonel already in his seventies. The colonel excelled in discipline, and he had great hopes as his grandson matured that the boy would carry on the family tradition. But for Charles such hopes were not sufficient to fill the yawning void he felt within. Lacking any wider purpose or ambition he turned increasingly to frivolous diversions and the indulgence of his considerable appetite. He had little interest in studies. Any religious faith he might once have known had been casually discarded along the way. Nevertheless, to oblige his grandfather he agreed to apply to the military academy of Saint-Cyr. With special tutoring he managed just to squeeze through the entrance examinations — allowance being made for his family name. No special connections, however, could help him squeeze his overfed body into a regulation uniform. For this a private tailor was commissioned. As a result, in years to come, even when he had become a scrawny hermit, he would be affectionately known by his comrades in the elite officer corps as "Piggy."

Charles looked resplendent in his uniform. But the uniform did not make the cadet. His years in the academy were distinguished only by the frequency of his official reprimands. It might be supposed that such a figure would earn the disdain of the more disciplined cadets. In fact he carried

off his escapades with such *joie d'esprit* that he seems instead to have endeared himself to his classmates, many of
whom would remain his lifelong friends. As one of them later
recalled, "If you have not seen Foucauld in his room, clad
in his white flannel pajamas buttoned with frogs, sprawled
leisurely on his divan or in a commodious armchair, enjoying a tasty snack of *pâté de fois gras,* washing it down with
a choice champagne, then you have never seen a man really
enjoying himself."

By this time, following his grandfather's death, Charles
had come into a considerable fortune — the better to un-
derwrite his epicurean tastes. His room became the site of
extravagant entertainments. He was generous in sharing the
contents of his wine cellar and the services of his personal
barber. But occasionally he went too far. One time he slipped
off base in disguise, defying a confinement to quarters, in
order to keep a dinner engagement with his mistress, a certain Mimi. When the ruse was discovered and he faced his
superiors he explained that he could hardly do otherwise —
a commitment to a young woman was a matter of honor.
This was not the military definition of honor, but for sheer
audacity it apparently won passing marks. He managed to
escape with a severe reprimand.

From Saint-Cyr Charles was passed on to cavalry school.
There he graduated in 1879, eighty-sixth in a class of eighty-
seven. The inspector general described him as "a remarkable
person...with no thought for anything except entertain-
ment." His first posting was to North Africa, where he
quickly got into trouble for sending Mimi on ahead, passing her off as the Viscountess de Foucauld. In light of the
ensuing scandal Charles was informed that he must make
a choice — either Mimi or the army. Without hesitation he
made his choice: he resigned his commission and returned

to France and to his scandalized family. They retaliated by putting his finances into the hands of a trustee.

He had scarcely arrived in Paris, however, when he applied to rejoin his old unit. News had reached him that his comrades were about to go into battle against Arab rebels and he could not bear the thought of sitting on the sidelines. And so he bade farewell to Mimi — this time forever — and returned to Algeria.

This was to be the turning point for Foucauld, the moment when a different side of his personality began to emerge. To everyone's surprise, he fought valiantly in battle and demonstrated considerable skill as an officer. The more lasting effect of this experience, however, was a new fascination with the North African desert and its people. After only six months in active service, long enough to rehabilitate his honor, Charles again resigned his commission to pursue an ambitious and dangerous mission. He had decided to undertake a one-man geographical expedition to Morocco, a vast territory as yet unexplored by Western outsiders. Because of the risks facing any lone Christian in this Muslim country, Charles disguised himself as a wandering Jewish rabbi. For eleven months he traveled the country, armed only with a sextant and compass, finally emerging with the material for a book. When it was published in 1885 he was awarded the gold medal of the French Geographical Society.

Back in Paris Charles's family was delighted by his new evidence of discipline and purpose. But already his restless heart was stirring in a new direction. The experience of Muslim piety had made a lasting impression on Charles, and he found himself increasingly drawn to the religion of his youth. As he wrote, "My exposure to this faith [Islam] and to the soul living always in God's presence helped me understand that there is something greater and more real than the pleasures of this world."

An irresistible force was drawing him, where he could not say. But over and over, as he restlessly roamed the streets of Paris, he repeated a prayer: "My God, if you exist, make your existence known to me." In the fall of 1886, after finally overcoming his inhibitions, he made his way to the church of St. Augustine, where he sought out Abbé Huvelin, a famous confessor and spiritual director. Finding Huvelin in his confessional he described his predicament and asked the priest to recommend some Christian reading. Huvelin, with inspired insight into the character of this seeker, told Charles that what he needed was not to be found in books. All that he needed to do was make his confession, receive communion, and he would believe. Charles complied, and at once he felt his life transformed. He left the church that day determined to give himself entirely to God. As he wrote later, "As soon as I believed there was a God, I understood that I could not do anything other than live for him. My religious vocation dates from the same moment as my faith."

The question for Charles now was what form this vocation should take. At the suggestion of Huvelin — into whose hands he fully entrusted himself — Charles undertook a pilgrimage to the Holy Land. There he spent several months visiting the holy shrines and following the footsteps of Jesus in the actual towns and countryside where he had walked. This experience would ultimately have a decisive impact on his life. But all that was clear at this point was his determination to embrace a life of prayer and poverty. The austere Trappist order seemed to offer the best means of fulfilling this calling. And so Charles renounced his fortune, applied to the Trappists, and eventually settled in a monastery in Syria, the most remote and impoverished community he could find.

Charles dutifully applied himself to the discipline of monastic life. He stuck it out for over seven years. But it did not satisfy his yearning. For one thing it fell short of his imagined ideal of poverty. Despite the famous rigors of the Trappist life, Charles found it altogether too comfortable. "We are poor in the eyes of the rich," he wrote, "but not so poor as Our Lord was." When a papal order slightly mitigated the Trappist dietary rules to allow a bit of oil or butter on their vegetables, Charles was indignant: "A little less mortification means so much less offered to the Good Lord; a little more spent on feeding us means so much less to give the poor. . . . Where will it all stop?" When he was once sent on a pastoral errand to the hovel of an Arab Christian who was dying of cholera, Charles was appalled to acknowledge the contrast between the dignified simplicity of the monastery and the actual poverty of a common peasant.

At the same time Charles had begun to question whether it was really to any traditional monastic life that he was called. Increasingly he was haunted by an insight from his sojourn in the Holy Land. What impressed him then was the realization that Jesus, though the Son of God, had lived most of his life as a poor man and a worker. As a carpenter in Nazareth Jesus had, in these lowly circumstances, embodied the Gospel message in its entirety, before ever announcing it in words. From this insight it occurred to Charles that the "hidden life" of Nazareth, and not the monastery, should be the model for his own spirituality.

It took a while for Charles to obtain a dispensation from the Trappists; he was at this point within months of making his final vows. Huvelin, too, was reluctant to endorse Charles's impetuous plan. But eventually Charles was free to return to the Holy Land, to Nazareth itself, where he found a position as a servant at a convent of Poor Clares. Calling himself simply Brother Charles, he spent three happy years in this occupation, dividing his waking hours between his minimal chores and a far more rigorous schedule of prayer. He exulted in the thought that he was living in the same place where Jesus had spent thirty years of his life and where "I have now the unutterable, the inexpressibly profound happiness of raking manure."

But though Charles aspired to emulate the "hidden life" of Jesus, his evident holiness eventually attracted the attention of the mother superior of the Poor Clares. She convinced Charles that he had a more important mission to perform in the world and urged him to become a priest. Though Charles felt unworthy of ordination, he found himself exhilarated by the dream of founding a community of likeminded brothers. Once again Charles turned to the counsel of Huvelin, who expressed his opinion in blunt terms: "You are not made, *not at all made,* to lead others." Nevertheless he helped arrange for Charles to return to France to undergo seminary training.

Shortly after his ordination in 1901 Charles returned once more to North Africa. To enact his new mission, he had concluded, it was no longer necessary to live in the actual town of Nazareth. "Nazareth" might be any place. And so he returned to Algeria, to the oasis of Béni-Abbès on the border of Morocco. His goal was to develop a new model of contemplative religious life, a community of "Little Brothers," who would live among the poor in a spirit of service and solidarity. In the constitutions he devised for his planned order he wrote, "The whole of our existence, the whole of our lives should cry the Gospel from the rooftops ... not by our words but by our lives." He was now forty-two, ready at last to begin his true mission.

Béni-Abbès was a predominantly Arab settlement, though

also the site of a French garrison. As a French colony Algeria was administered under military authority. Since it was the policy of the French government to avoid any provocation of the Muslim population, Charles could hardly have established his hermitage without approval from the military authorities. But here, and not for the last time, his old connections proved invaluable. Many of his classmates from the academy had risen to positions of authority in the colonies, and they were only too willing to assist a former comrade — even one whose career had taken such an unlikely turn.

Ostensibly Charles's mission was to divide his time between service to the Arabs and pastoral duties among the garrisoned troops. He was the only priest within 250 miles. Thus, a good deal of his time was spent saying Mass and hearing confessions from the soldiers. But his heart was with the mass of his Arab neighbors to whom Christ was as yet unknown. He dressed like one of them in a coarse, white robe, with a leather belt around his waist. His only distinguishing marks were the rosary tucked in his belt and an emblem of his own design — a red heart with a cross — sewn over his breast. His aim was not to convert the Arabs, but rather to offer a Christian presence in their midst.

Ultimately Charles regarded himself as simply the advance agent for a community of Little Brothers. But no followers ever came. There were not many at the time who could even comprehend his novel approach to mission; fewer still who could endure the extreme, nearly impossible, standards of asceticism that Charles embraced. He had traveled far from the days when he had lounged on a sofa, feasting on oysters and pâté. Now he worked hard by day, spent half the night in prayer, slept on the bare ground, and subsisted on a diet of dates and boiled barley. His former abbot, one of those to whom he frequently appealed for helpers, was realistic to observe, "I fear he would drive a disciple mad by excessive mental concentration before killing him by excessive austerities."

After several years in Béni-Abbès Charles began to find the isolated outpost too congested for his taste. In 1905, on the lookout for a more remote setting, he accepted an invitation from Colonel Henri Laperrine, an old classmate and now the commander of the Saharan Oases, to tag along on an expedition to the Saharan interior. Thus Charles discovered the rugged Hoggar region — a barren plateau surrounded by dramatic volcanic mountains, deep in the heart of the desert. Charles was enchanted by the complete isolation of the region and by its mysterious inhabitants, the Tuaregs. They were a semi-nomadic people, famous for their ardor in battle, easily recognized by their peculiar complexion, their skin dyed blue from the color of their distinctive veils. If he were to live here he would be the only priest within sixty days of desert travel. The attraction was irresistible. He decided at once to move his hermitage here to the village of Tamanrasset. Laperrine, for his part, had hoped for such an outcome; it pleased him to imagine that through this priest a bridge might be formed to the remote tribal peoples of the Saharan interior. Who was better equipped for such a mission than Piggy?

His new home, Tamanrasset, was hardly a village at all. Twenty families lived in this settlement, halfway up a mountain at an elevation of 4600 feet. A small oasis nourished a few tufts of grass and sustained the meager gardens and small herds of goats on which the people subsisted. By day the sun was mercilessly bright with temperatures reaching 110 degrees. At sunset the mountain tops caught fire in a crimson blaze. By night the temperature could drop seventy degrees, while the sky was illuminated by a sea of stars. With time Charles came to know that sky so well that he could better navigate in the dark than he could by daylight.

Choosing a spot just out of sight of his neighbors, he built himself a house of stones and reeds. It consisted of two rooms, each about six by nine feet and a little over six feet high. Ever hopeful regarding the arrival of fresh recruits, Charles eventually constructed a "refectory" and "parlor" and a series of additional cells, each of the same claustrophobic dimensions. At the center of it all, when he was finished, was a burning lamp, indicating the presence of the Eucharist — to the eyes of faith, the very presence of Christ himself, here among the most abandoned and neglected. Charles spent hours each day prostrate before that lamp and the box beside it. Meanwhile his letters, filled with chatty details of his daily life and spiritual reflections, were punctuated by the plaintive appeal: "My only regret is that I am still alone.... Try to send me some brothers.... I would so love to have a companion who would be my successor...." But this was not to be.

The years passed. Foucauld grew older. The plump young cadet had given way to a gaunt figure of middle age, bearded, almost bald, his skin darkened by the sun. His smile revealed missing teeth, while his eyes burned with a passionate intensity. From the time of his arrival in the Hoggar he had struggled hard to master the Tuareg language. The fruit of his study was recorded in a massive Tuareg dictionary, a manuscript completed shortly before his death and later found among his papers. Otherwise it was a life spent with little sign of outward accomplishment.

Nevertheless, as he wrote to a friend, "Living alone in the country is a good thing; one can act, even without doing much, because one becomes one of them. One is approachable, because one is so small." It was thus a fruitful loneliness, a way of being available to his neighbors. He had little to offer them but his friendship, his care, and occasional medicines. They had no use for his religion. But having overcome their initial suspicions of this strange foreigner who had traveled so far to share their poverty, Charles was accepted by the people of Tamanrasset. From there, by the ancient channels of bedouin communication, his reputation extended throughout the Hoggar.

In 1908, after two years in Tamanrasset, Foucauld obtained a dispensation from the Vatican to say Mass by himself, without a server, as well as permission to construct a tabernacle for the reserved Eucharist. And so he was not entirely alone. "To receive the grace of God," he wrote to a Trappist, "you must go to a desert place and stay a while. There you can be emptied and unburdened of everything that does not pertain to God. There the house of our soul is swept clean to make room for God alone to dwell.... We need this silence, this absence of every creature, so that God can build his hermitage within us."

The spiritual path of Charles de Foucauld was modeled on the hidden life of Jesus in Nazareth, a way of constant abandonment to the love of God, whether in the silence of desert spaces or in the midst of others. There is no doubt that in embarking on this path Foucauld prepared himself to give everything and that he carefully calculated the cost. Already in 1897, while living in Nazareth, he had written in his journal:

Think that you are going to die a martyr, stripped of everything, stretched out on the ground, naked, hardly recognizable, covered with blood and wounds, violently and painfully killed ... and wish it to be today.... Think of this death often, prepare yourself for it and judge things at their true value.

It was a remarkably prophetic meditation. Was it also evidence of a morbid imagination? If so, it was a natural feature of a spirituality centered so closely on the imitation of Christ. "We cannot possibly love him without imitating him," he wrote. "Since he suffered and died in agony, we cannot love him and yet want to be crowned with roses while he was crowned with thorns. . . . We must love him just as he loved us, in the very same way."

All the same, it seems that for Foucauld the consciousness of impending sacrifice grew over time to a steady conviction. Scattered throughout his journals one finds such statements as these: "To prepare oneself constantly for martyrdom, and accept it without a shadow of reluctance, like the divine Lamb, in Jesus, through Jesus, for Jesus." "I must try and live as if I were to die a martyr today. Every minute I must imagine I am going to be martyred this very evening." And in a booklet found on his body on the day he died: "My wish is to live as if I were to die a martyr today. . . . "

Foucauld was granted this wish; so he lived, and so he died. And yet is it entirely accurate to describe Foucauld as a martyr? Among the motivations of those who killed him it is possible to discern a variety of factors beyond simple "hatred for the faith." But this is undoubtedly true with most martyrs, whose witness to Christ is inevitably complicated by cultural, ethnic, or political interests. As for Charles de Foucauld, it must be acknowledged that, despite his desire to live a hidden life as a brother to the Tuaregs, he was finally unable to obliterate his identity as a son of France and a former officer.

Foucauld deplored certain features of colonial rule, especially the failure of French authorities to check the ongoing commerce of slavery. But he continued to affirm an idealistic notion of France's role in bringing civilization and Christian morality to the benighted peoples of the Sahara. His criticism of colonial policy was that it failed to reflect its exalted purpose. As he wrote to a friend,

> I suffer as a Frenchman to see the natives not being ruled as they ought. On the contrary, the moral and spiritually inadequate condition of these peoples is made all the worse by treating them as no more than a means of material acquisition. What the natives learn from the infidel Frenchmen who proclaim the doctrine of "fraternity" is neglect, or ambition, or greed, and from almost everyone, unfortunately, indifference, aversion and harsh behavior.

In another place he wrote, "If we act according to our lights, if we civilize instead of exploiting, in fifty years Algeria, Tunis and Morocco will be an extension of France. If we do not live up to our duty, if we exploit rather than civilize, we will lose everything and the union we have created from these diverse peoples will turn against us."

Throughout his years in North Africa Foucauld maintained friendly relations with the army. In a sense he had no other choice if he were to pursue his mission. But at the same time many of the officers were truly old friends from his earlier life. They consulted him about conditions in the interior, and he readily provided intelligence about the terrain, about the best location for encampments, and about the dangers of bandits and rebels. The army in turn regarded him as a kind of French agent in the Hoggar. It was a role Charles did not positively decline.

The outbreak of World War I, which intensified conflicts

between the army and rebel tribesmen, enhanced Charles's value to the colonial enterprise. Many of his army friends were recalled to the trenches in Europe, and Charles himself inquired about the chances of serving as a stretcher bearer. It was his old friend — now General — Laperrine who instructed him otherwise: "Stay in the Hoggar. We need you there." And so in his own corner of the world Charles was prepared to do his part.

In April 1916 a French stronghold at Djanet on the Libyan frontier fell to an army of Senoussi rebels. The Senoussi were a brotherhood of Muslim nationalists, drawn from a number of ethnic groups, united in their determination to drive the foreign infidels from the land of Islam. Warned that the Senoussi were drawing near to Tamanrasset, Charles decided to build a small fortress. Using local materials over a period of months he managed to raise a formidable structure with walls a solid meter thick. He finished the fortification on November 15. Visiting officers were impressed and asked his permission to store supplies and weapons inside. Foucauld raised no objection.

It is difficult today to reconcile the image of Foucauld the French patriot with the image of Charles, the Little Brother of Jesus. By the same token one can imagine with what ease the Senoussi warriors who broke into his fort on December 1, who bound his arms, shot him, and left him bleeding in the sand, might confuse the holy *Marabout* for a representative of France. For their careless violence they were rewarded with the contents of his fort. Aside from supplies of food they recovered six cases of ammunition and thirty carbines. They left his Tuareg dictionary scattered in the courtyard, along with the apparently worthless Tabernacle, not to mention his body, all discovered later by French troops. Such are the complexities of Charles de Foucauld and the ambiguities of his death. By the end he had managed to combine the heroic ideals of both his grandfather the colonel and his pious mother, all reflected in the family motto: Never Retreat.

Foucauld himself was aware of the ironies of his existence. Daily he confronted the weakness of his faith and the ambiguities of his witness. In the end those ambiguities ran deeper than he could acknowledge. But he prayed that if he made his small offering in love then God would purify his intentions and bring forth the harvest from his small seeds. Ultimately, the meaning of his life, distilled with the passage of time, had nothing to do with carbines, forts, the honor of France, or even the matter of his death, but with the spiritual vision he summarized toward the end of his life:

> Jesus came to Nazareth, the place of the hidden life, of ordinary life, of family life, of prayer, work, obscurity, silent virtues, practiced with no witnesses other than God, his friends and neighbors. Nazareth, the place where most people lead their lives. We must infinitely respect the least of our brothers ... let us mingle with them. Let us be one of them to the extent that God wishes ... and treat them fraternally in order to have the honor and joy of being accepted as one of them.

Failing the joy of being accepted as one of them, there was another joy. On the last day of his life he wrote a letter to his cousin Marie, which was left sealed and ready for the mailman:

> Our annihilation is the most powerful means that we have of uniting ourselves to Jesus. One finds one doesn't love enough, that is true, but Almighty God, who knows with what he has molded us, and who loves us

much more than a mother can love her child, has said that he will not cast out those who come to him.

At that point he heard the knock on the door, the sound for which he had trained his ear: "Illness, danger, the prospect of death, it is the call. 'Here is the Spouse: go forth to meet him.' "

For Further Reference on the Life of Charles de Foucauld

Charles Hillyer, *Charles de Foucauld* (Collegeville, Minn.: Liturgical Press, 1990).

Charles Lepetit, *Two Dancers in the Desert: The Life of Charles de Foucauld* (Tunbridge Wells: Burns & Oates, and Maryknoll, N.Y.: Orbis Books, 1983).

A Little Brother of Jesus, *Silent Pilgrimage to God: The Spirituality of Charles de Foucauld* (London: Darton, Longman and Todd, and Maryknoll, N.Y.: Orbis Books, 1974).

Marion Mill Preminger, *The Sands of Tamanrasset* (New York: Hawthorn Books, 1961).

Jean-François Six, ed., *Spiritual Autobiography of Charles de Foucauld* (New York: P. J. Kenedy & Sons, 1964).

Jean-François Six, *Witness in the Desert: The Life of Charles de Foucauld* (New York: Macmillan, 1965).

Margaret Trouncer, *Charles de Foucauld* (London: George G. Harrap, 1972).

Myself and My Past Life:
The Mercy of God

*As soon as I believed there was a God, I understood
that I could not do anything other than live for him.
My religious vocation dates from the same moment as
my faith.*   — August 14, 1901

*From the time of his conversion in October 1886 Charles de
Foucauld was driven by a powerful sense of vocation — a
sense that he had been called by God for some unique purpose and mission. In retrospect he was able to discern in his
past life the hand of Providence drawing him, through so
many unlikely twists and turns, toward his true end. And
yet the struggle to find his calling was marked by years of
trial and error. His only certainty was that he was called to
imitate, as nearly as possible, the life of Jesus of Nazareth.
This conviction led him initially to a Trappist monastery in
Syria, where he remained for seven years (1890–97). Ultimately, compelled by the same spirit that had driven him
to the Trappists — the desire for perfect poverty and obscurity — he departed the monastery and set out for the Holy
Land. There, in Nazareth, the very town where Jesus had*

spent the better part of his life, he found work as a servant to a convent of Poor Clares.

Foucauld left few autobiographical writings. Among these, however, are the following notes, written during a retreat in 1897, which give a partial account of the path to Nazareth.

•

O God, we should all hymn the praises of your mercies — we, who were all created for everlasting glory and redeemed by the blood of Jesus, by your blood, my Lord Jesus, beside me now in the tabernacle. But if we all have cause to do so, then how much the more have I? From my childhood I have been surrounded by so many graces: the son of a saintly mother, who learned from her to know you, to love you, and, as soon as I could speak at all, to pray to you....

And the true piety of my upbringing!...I see myself going to church with my father (and how long ago that is!), and with my grandfather. I see grandmother and my cousins going to Mass every day. And my first Holy Communion, after a long and careful preparation, surrounded by the blessings and encouragement of a family wholly Christian, in the presence of those I loved best in all the world, so that on a single day there came together everything necessary to let me taste pure joy....

And then, when alas, despite so many blessings, I began to drift away from you, how gently you used my grandfather's voice to call me back to you. With what mercy you restrained me from falling into the ultimate excesses by keeping tenderness toward him alive in my heart. But alas, in spite of everything, I withdrew even further from you, my Lord and my Life, and my life began to be a death, or rather, had already become a death in your eyes.

Yet in that state of death, you preserved me still, keeping the memories of past times alive in my soul, together with esteem for what was good, and an attachment, dormant yet still alive like the glow of fire under the ashes, to certain beautiful and devout souls, and respect for the Catholic faith and the religious life. All my faith had vanished, but respect and esteem were still there, untouched. And you gave me other graces too, O God: you kept alive in me the taste for study, for serious reading and good things, and with it a disgust for vice and shame. I did evil, but I never approved of it or loved it.

You made me experience a melancholic emptiness, a sadness that I never felt at other times. It would come back to me every evening when I was alone in my rooms; it kept me silent and depressed during our so-called celebrations: I would organize them, but when the time came, I went through them in silence, disgust, and infinite boredom. You gave me the ill-defined unrest that marks an unquiet conscience which, though it may be wholly asleep, is not completely dead. I never felt that sadness, that distress, that restlessness apart from those times. It was undoubtedly a gift from you, O God. How far off I was in my doubting! How good you are!...

And while you were thus protecting me, time passed, until the moment came when you judged it right to bring me back into the fold. In spite of me, you dissolved all the evil relationships that would have kept me away from you. You even unloosed all those good ties that would have prevented me from returning to the bosom of my family, where you willed that I should find salvation, but which would have prevented me from one day living for you alone. At the same time, you gave me a life of serious studies, an obscure life in solitude and poverty. In heart and mind I was still far from you, yet I had begun to live in a less vicious atmosphere; it was neither true light nor goodness — that was lacking — but it was not so deep a morass nor so odious a wickedness. Little by little the place was swept clean; the flood still covered the earth, but the waters were continually falling, and it had stopped raining. You had broken down the barriers, softened my soul, prepared the ground by burning off the thorns and bushes....

And having cleansed the filth from my soul and entrusted it to your angels, you, O God, planned to reenter it yourself — for even after having received so many graces, it still did not acknowledge you.... Then you breathed into it a taste for virtue, the virtue of the pagans: you let me search through the works of the pagan philosophers, and I found nothing there but emptiness and disgust. Next you let me glance at a few pages of a Christian book, and you made me conscious of its warmth and beauty. You made me realize that I might find there, if not truth (for I did not believe that men can know truth), at least the elements of virtue, and you inspired me to look for instruction in a virtue completely pagan in Christian books. Thus you brought to me an awareness of the mysteries of religion....

By the beginning of October 1886, after six months of family life, I admired virtue and longed for it, but I still did not know you. By what devices, O God of goodness, you made yourself known to me! What devices did you not use? What exterior means, both gentle and strong? What an astonishing series of circumstances, in which everything combined to drive me toward you: unexpected solitude, my emotions, the sickness of those dear to me, ardent feelings, a return to Paris as the result of a surprising event. And what interior graces: the need for solitude, recollection, and pious reading; the urge I felt to go into your churches — I who did not believe in you; my unrest of soul, my anguish; my search for truth; my prayer: "O God, if you exist, let me know of your existence." All these things were your work, O God — the work of you alone.

A noble soul supported you — by its silence, its gentleness, its goodness and perfection. It let itself be seen; it was good and it spread its seductive perfume around itself, but it never intruded itself. It was you, O Jesus, my Savior, who did all things, both within and without. You attracted me to virtue through a soul in which virtue seemed so beautiful to me that it snatched away my heart irrecoverably. Through that same soul, you also attracted me to truth. Then you gave me four blessings. First, you inspired me with the thought that as this soul was so intelligent, the religion it believed so firmly could not be the folly I had thought it. Second, you inspired me with another idea: since this religion is not folly, may it not be that there is to be found in it that truth which is to be found in no other upon earth, nor yet in any system of philosophy?

Your third blessing was to say to me: Study this religion, then — put yourself under a teacher of the Catholic religion, a learned priest, and see what there is in it, and if you find yourself compelled to believe what it teaches. And the fourth was the unparalleled blessing of directing me for my instruction in religion to Father Huvelin. I believe, O God, that by leading me to go into his confessional on one of the last days of that October...you were giving me the best of all good things. If there is joy in heaven at the repentance of a sinner, then how great joy there must have been when I entered his confessional! What a blessed day that was — a day of blessing. And since that day my whole life has been a chain of blessings.

You put me under the wing of a saint, and I have stayed

there. You used his hands to bear me up, and the result has been grace upon grace. I asked for instruction in religion: he made me get down on my knees and make my confession and sent me straight away to Holy Communion. When I think of it, I cannot stop myself from crying: and I do not want to stop the tears running down for, O God, they are so justified. What streams of tears should flow from my eyes at the remembrance of so many mercies! How good you have been — how happy I am! What have I done to deserve it? ...

How good you are, my God, to have broken everything around me, to have annihilated in such a way everything that would have prevented me living for you alone, giving me an ever deeper feeling of the futility and falseness of the life of the world, and of the vast distance there is between the perfect life, the life of the Gospel, and the life men lead in the world. You gave me a tender and increasing love for you, O Lord Jesus, and a taste for prayer, trust in your word, a profound awareness of the duty of almsgiving, a longing to imitate you. You gave me too those words in a sermon of Father Huvelin's which are now so indelibly engraved on my soul: "May you so truly have taken the lowest place that no one will ever be able to take it from you," and a thirst to give you the greatest sacrifice I am capable of making for you, by leaving forever the family which had been also my joy, to live and die far away from it. You gave me my search for a life like yours, in which I might share completely in your abjection, your poverty, your humble work, your obscurity — the search made so clear to me in a last retreat at Clamart.

On January 15, 1890, I was enabled to make this sacrifice, and I received from your hand that grace, La Trappe: daily Communion; all I learned in seven years spent in the religious life.... After three and a half years spent in waiting, the most reverend General told me, on January 23, 1897,

that it was the will of God that I should follow that in
me which was driving me out of the Trappist order into
a life of poverty, humble labor, and profound obscurity —
the life whose vision had been with me so long. There followed my departure for the Holy Land, my pilgrimage and
arrival at Nazareth. The first Wednesday I spent there you let
me, O God, through the intercession of St. Joseph, to enter
the convent of St. Clare as a servant. O the peace, happiness, consolation, blessings, and wonderful happiness I knew
there! ...

I can only fall far short of such mercies, O God: I can
only beseech the Blessed Virgin and all devout souls to give
thanks for me, for I am overwhelmed by blessings. O beloved
Bridegroom, what have you not done for me? What do you
want from me? What do you expect from me, that you have
so overwhelmed me? O God, give yourself thanks through
me, create remembrance, gratitude, fidelity, and love in me; I
am overcome, I fail, O God; create my thoughts, words, and
deeds, so that they may all give you thanks and glorify you
in me. Amen. Amen. Amen.   — SA 10–18

•

In this second text, a letter written on August 14, 1901, Fou-
cauld again describes his spiritual journey, this time on the
eve of his return to the Sahara.

As soon as I believed there was a God, I understood that I
could not do anything other than live for him. My religious
vocation dates from the same moment as· my faith. How
great God is! There is such a difference between God and
everything that is not him!

In its beginnings my faith had a good many obstacles to
conquer. I had doubted so much that I didn't believe every-

thing in a day. First it was the miracles in the Gospel that I
considered unbelievable. Then it was that I wanted to mix in
passages of the Koran with my prayers. But God's grace and
my confessor's advice cleared away the fog.

I wanted to be a religious and to live for God alone.
I wanted to do the most perfect thing whatever it might
be. My confessor made me wait three years. As for myself,
though I longed to "breathe out my life before God in sheer
losing of myself," as Bossuet says, I did not know what order
to choose. The Gospel showed me that "the first command-
ment is to love God with all your heart," and that everything
had to be enfolded in love. Everyone knows that love's first
effect is imitation. Therefore I was to enter the order where I
would find the most exact imitation of JESUS. I didn't feel I
was made to imitate his public life of preaching: thus I ought
to imitate his hidden life as a poor and humble workman at
Nazareth. It seemed to me that no one offered me this life
better than the Trappists.

I loved very fondly what family the Lord had left me. I
wanted to make a sacrifice, to be like him who made so
many, and I left home — it's been nearly twelve years ago
now — for a Trappist monastery in Armenia. I spent six and
a half years there. Then, desiring a deeper dispossession and
a greater lowliness so that I might be still more like Jesus,
I went to Rome and received permission from the superior
general of the order to go to Nazareth and live there without
anyone knowing who I was, as a workman living by my daily
labor. I stayed there four years, withdrawn from the world in
a blessed solitude and inward prayerfulness, tasting the joys
of that poverty and lowliness God had made me desire so ardently in order that I might imitate him. Exactly a year ago
I took the road back for France on my confessor's advice in
order to receive holy orders. I was just ordained a priest, and

I'm applying now to go to the Sahara where I would continue "the hidden life of Jesus at Nazareth." I don't mean to preach but to live in the solitude, the poverty, and the humble labor of Jesus, while trying to do good to souls not with my words but with prayer, the offering of the Holy Sacrifice, penance, and the practice of charity.   — CG 37–38

Chapter 1

Hidden Life

I do not think there is a Gospel phrase which has made a deeper impression on me and transformed my life more than this one: "Insofar as you did this to one of the least of these brothers of mine, you did it to me." One has only to think that these words were spoken by the uncreated Truth, who also said, "This is my body... this is my blood..." to be kindled into searching for Jesus and loving him in the "least of these brothers of mine," these sinners, these poor people.

—August 1, 1916

From his experience in the Holy Land, Foucauld derived one essential insight: that Jesus, though divine, had spent most of his life in complete obscurity. This insight became the key not only to his interpretation of the Gospel but to his own personal vocation. Again and again in his meditations he returned to the humility and love of God who assumed our frail humanity. Even in the Incarnation, God spurned all worldly status and assumed the lowliest position, that of a common carpenter in an insignificant town. Christ's life began in a manger in Bethlehem and ended on the cross of Calvary. In the same spirit of humility he left himself to us

41

both in the Eucharist, our spiritual food, and in the needs of
the poor, our neighbors ("Insofar as you did this to one of
the least of these my brothers of mine, you did it to me").
To imitate Christ, Foucauld was convinced, one must begin
by contemplating these mysteries and embracing the spirit of
the hidden life.

IN HIS FOOTSTEPS

Meditation in Nazareth

[*Christ says to him:*] "Look at the life I have fashioned for
you: could it possibly parallel my hidden life more perfectly?
You enjoy it in sum and in its least details. In the Trappist order the resemblance was not close enough for you.
But how perfectly it is now yours! How well I have treated
you! You are living it at Nazareth, unknown, inordinately
poor, lowly in your smock and sandals, a poor servant to
poor nuns. Some take you for a laborer of the lowest kind;
others think you are an outcast; some think you are perhaps the son of a criminal. Most — nearly all, in fact — take
you for a fool. You obey the nuns and the portresses as I
obeyed my parents. You give orders to nobody, absolutely
no one. You work, doing what you are told sometimes by
one person, sometimes by another, never doing anything for
yourself, nothing you yourself choose to do. Your time is divided, as mine used to be, between work, prayer, and sacred
reading. It is split up as mine was, in just the way you think
comes closest to my way of doing things, and in obedience
to your director, who has given his approval of our division
of it into prayer, reading, and work. 'He that heareth him,
heareth me' [Luke 10:16]. You are following me in all things

by obeying my Father by always obeying your director, who tells you to do what I did, to be what I was, to live as I lived, to be a reflection of me in every way, in the place where you live, the life you lead, and above all in your soul."

—June 17, 1898, SA 47–48

•

My God, from the depths of your mercy, from the treasury of your mystical and infinite goodness, you have given me the great grace of living under that sky and in that land where you lived, of walking over the very ground you walked over — and, alas, watered with your tears, sweat, and blood. Do not leave me tearless as I visit the places that witnessed your sufferings; do not leave me tearless when I kiss the path your footsteps trod in Gethsemane, along the Way of Sorrows, to the praetorium and Calvary. Give me a heart of flesh in place of my heart of stone, and because you have given me this inexpressible grace, let me kiss this most holy soil, let me kiss it with my heart and my soul, and with the tears you want me to have, the tears I ought to have, O my Lord, my King, my Master, my Beloved, my Savior, my God!

—Retreat at Nazareth, November 1898, SA 92–93

The Visitation

[*Jesus speaks:*] "I had scarcely taken flesh when I asked my Mother to take me to the house where John was to be born, so that I might sanctify him before his birth. In the Incarnation, I gave myself to the world for its salvation. Even before my birth I was working at my task, the sanctification of mankind — and I moved my Mother to work at it with me. She is not the only one I have ever moved to work

at the sanctification of souls from the first moment of being given to them: I do the same in every soul to which I
give myself. On one occasion I said to my apostles, 'Preach,'
and I gave them their mission and laid down rules for their
fulfillment of it.

"Here and now I am saying to other souls — to all those
who have been given me and now lead hidden lives, possessing me without having been given a mission to preach — I tell
them to sanctify souls by silently carrying me among them.
To souls in silence, leading the hidden life in solitude far from
the world, I say, 'All, all, of you, work for the sanctification
of the world; work in the world as my Mother did, wordlessly, silently; go and set up your devotional retreats in the
midst of those who do not know me; carry me among them
by setting up an altar among them, a tabernacle, carrying the
Gospel to them not by word of mouth but by the persuasive
force of example, not by speaking, but by living; sanctify the
world, carry me into the world, all you pious souls living a
hidden and silent life — as Mary carried me to John.' "
— Eight Days in Ephraim, 1898, SA 79–80

The Nativity and Circumcision

[*Jesus speaks:*] "I was born, born for you, in a cave, in December, in the cold, homeless, in the middle of a winter's
night, in the unheard-of poverty of the extremely poor, in
solitude, in an abandonment unique in this world. What, my
children, do I want you to learn from my birth? *To believe in
my love,* to believe that I have loved you until now. To hope
in me, who have loved you so dearly. I want to teach you to
despise the world, which was so unimportant to me. I want
to teach you *poverty, lowliness, solitude, humility, penance.*
I want to teach you to love me, for I was not content with

giving myself to the world in the Incarnation, sanctifying it invisibly in the Visitation; no, that did not satisfy my love. From the moment of my birth onward, I showed myself to you, giving myself wholly to you, putting myself in your hands. From then on, you could touch me, hear me, possess me, serve me, console me. Love me now; I am so close to you.

"In my unimaginable goodness, I did not merely give myself to you at my birth for a few hours or years: I am still in your hands, and shall be henceforth until the end of the world. Think of the unending good fortune I brought you in my birth: the ability to *serve me* — to serve me by serving the Church, to serve me by serving your neighbor, to serve me myself, living there near you in the tabernacle. Not only can you serve me, you can also *console* me. I watched you at every moment of your life, at every moment of my own, and my human Heart, which loves you so fondly, has rejoiced or suffered at each of these moments, rejoicing if they were devoted to good, suffering if they were used to do evil.

"How happy you should be to be able to console me at every moment of your lives! By becoming so small, so gentle a child, I was crying out to you: *Have trust! Come close to me!* Do not be afraid of me, come to me, take me in your arms, adore me. But when you adore me, give me what children need; loving embraces. Do not be afraid, do not be so frightened in the presence of such a gentle baby, smiling at you and holding out his arms to you. He is your God, but he is all smiles and gentleness. Do not be afraid."
— Eight Days in Ephraim, 1898, SA 80–81

Jesus in His Incarnation and Birth

My God, all this happy day I shall meditate upon you. Yes, my God, you are constant and faithful. You still give me your

Grace. Your Saints and Angels still are helping me, only I myself am helpless. You urge me on to good and load me with graces, and everything is helping me in heaven and on earth, and I alone make obstacles through my cowardice and weakness and stupidity.

The Incarnation sprang from the goodness of God. The humility contained in this mystery is amazing, marvelous, astonishing. It shines with a dazzling brilliance. God, the Essence, the Infinite, Perfection, Creator, All-Powerful, the Great Sovereign Lord of All, becomes a man and takes on himself the body and soul of a man. He appears on earth as a man, and the humblest of men.

What is man's respect worth? Was it meant that God should seek to possess it? As he looks down upon the world from the height of his divinity all seem equal in his eyes, the great, the small, all like ants and worms to him. He disdained all false grandeur, which is in reality so very small, and had no wish to assume it himself. And as he came on earth to ransom us and teach us, he taught us from the very first, and all through his life, to despise human greatness and detach ourselves entirely from man's esteem. He was born, lived, and died in deepest abjection, in the lowest humiliation, for he took once for all the lowest place so completely that no one has ever humbled himself lower than he did. It was to teach us that he put himself last so constantly, and to show us that men and their respect are worth nothing; that we must never despise those living in meanness and that the abject need never grieve for their humiliation. They are near to God, near to the King of Kings. He teaches us that since our conversation is not of this world we should make no matter of the forms of this world, but live only for that heavenly kingdom which the God-man saw forever here below by the Beatific Vision, and which we should see always with the eyes of Faith, walking in this world as though we were not of this world, without concern of outside things and busy with one thing only, with contemplating and loving our Heavenly Father and doing his Will.

—Retreat at Nazareth, November 1897, MH 43–44

NAZARETH

The Hidden Life of Jesus

They returned into Galilee, to their city Nazareth.
—Luke 2:39

[*Jesus speaks:*] "After my presentation and my flight into Egypt, I withdrew to Nazareth. There I spent the years of my childhood and youth, till I was thirty years of age. Once again, it was for your sake I went there, *for love of you.* What was the meaning of that part of my life? I led it for your instruction. I instructed you continually for thirty years, not in words, but by my silence and example. What was it I was teaching you? I was teaching you primarily that it is possible to do good to men — great good, infinite good, divine good — without using words, without preaching, without fuss, but by silence and by giving them a good example. What kind of example? The example of devotion of duty toward God lovingly fulfilled, and goodness toward all men, loving kindness to those about one, and domestic duties fulfilled in holiness. The example of poverty, lowliness, recollection, withdrawal: the obscurity of a life hidden in God, a life of prayer, penance, and withdrawal, completely lost in God, buried deep in him. I was teaching you to live by the labor of your own hands, so as to be a burden on no one and to have something to give to the poor. And I was giving this way of life an incomparable beauty — the beauty of being a copy of mine.

"Everyone who wants to be perfect must live in *poverty,* imitating with the utmost fidelity my poverty at Nazareth. How clearly I preached *humility* at Nazareth, by spending thirty years in obscure labors, and *obscurity* by remaining so completely unknown for thirty years — I who am the light of the world — and *obedience,* in that I, who am God, made myself subject for thirty years to my parents who, although unquestionably holy, were human beings nonetheless. Having seen me so obedient so long to those to whom I owed no obedience whatsoever, whose sovereign Master, Creator, and Judge I was, how can you refuse perfect obedience to those of whom I, your God, have said: 'He that heareth you, heareth me'?

"*How little esteem I showed of the things of this world,* of human greatness, and the ways of the world, of everything the world holds dear: nobility, wealth, status, knowledge, cleverness, repute, honor, worldly distinction, good manners. I pushed all these things far away from me, so that I should be seen only as a poor laborer living very devoutly, completely withdrawn from the world."

—Eight Days in Ephraim, 1898, SA 82–84

•

My Jesus, you are so close to me: inspire in me the thoughts I should have about your hidden life.

"And he went down with them and came to Nazareth and was subject to them." He went down, he humbled himself — his life was one of humility. Being God, you took the appearance of a man; as a man, you made yourself the least of men. Your life was one of *lowliness:* the place you took was the lowest of all. You went down *with* them to live their

life with them, the life of the poor laborer, living by working. Your life, like theirs, was one of *work and poverty.* They
were obscure, and you lived in the shade of their *obscurity.*
You went to Nazareth, a forgotten little town, hidden in the
hills, from where, it was commonly said, nothing good ever
came. This was real withdrawal, far from the world and its
great cities. And you lived in this state of *retirement.*

You *were subject to them* — subject as a son is to his
father and mother. Your life was one of *submission,* filial
submission. You were obedient in every way that a good son
is obedient. If your parents had wanted anything that was
not in harmony with your divine vocation, you would not
have done it. You obeyed "God rather than men," as you
did when you remained behind in Jerusalem for three days.
But except when your vocation required you not to submit
yourself to their wishes, you were obedient to them in all
things; you were the best of sons in every way. Therefore
you were not only obedient to their least wishes, but you
forestalled them, doing whatever would please them, console
them, make their life pleasant and acceptable to them, striving with all your heart to make them happy, being a model
son, doing everything possible for them — insofar as your
vocation allowed. But your vocation was to perfection, and
you, O Son of God, could not be anything but perfect.

This was your life at Nazareth — here, where I have the
infinite good fortune, the unparalleled grace of living! For
this I render all my thanks.

Your life was that of a model among sons — and you lived
it with a mother and father who were both poor working
people. This was one half of your life, the part turned toward
the world while it filled heaven with a celestial perfume. It
was the visible part of your life. The invisible part was your
life in God, a life of unceasing contemplation. You worked,

consoled your parents, conversing with them with the utmost fondness and holiness, praying with them throughout
the day. But you prayed too in the solitude and darkness of
the night; your soul was poured out in silence.

You were always, always, praying, at every moment — for
to pray is to be with God, and you were God. But far into
the nights your human soul prolonged that contemplation,
and it was united closely at every moment of the day with
your divinity. Your life was one continual outpouring into
God, a continual gazing at God, unending contemplation of
God at every moment of your life.

And what kind of prayer was it that made up the half
of your life in Nazareth? First and above all it was *adoration,* that is, *contemplation,* that silent adoration which is
the most eloquent of prayers: *Tibi silentium laus* ["Silence is
praise to you"]. It was that kind of silent adoration which
confirms a declaration of love most passionately, just as love
expressed in wondering admiration is the most ardent love.

Then, secondly — in second place and occupying less
time — it was *thanksgiving:* thanksgiving first for the divine
glory, for the fact that God is God, then thanksgiving for the
graces bestowed on the world and all created things. Then
a cry for *forgiveness,* forgiveness for all the sins committed against God, forgiveness for those who do not ask for
it themselves, an act of contrition for the whole world, an
act of sorrow at seeing God offended. Then *petition,* asking
for the glory of God, that God might be glorified by all created things, that his reign among them might begin, that his
will might be done among them as it is among the angels,
and that these lowly creatures might be given everything,
whether spiritual or temporal, that they need, and might finally be freed from all evil both in this world and the next.
And petition, too, asking that graces might be poured es-

pecially abundantly on those who, by the divine will, lived close to Jesus and around him: his mother and father, his cousins and friends, those who loved him and clung to him.
— Retreat at Nazareth, November 1897, MH 84–86

Jesus' Public Life

My God, here am I at your feet in my cell, all around is in silence, all sleeps. I am perhaps the only soul in Nazareth, at this moment, at your feet. What have I done to merit this grace? Thank you, thank you. I am grateful. I adore you from the depths of my soul. I am yours and only yours. All my being is yours: it is of necessity without any will of mine, but also it is so voluntary, with all my heart's will. Do with me what you will. Let me make this retreat as you wish. "Be you perfect as your Father in heaven is perfect," you answer. Ah! Then, my God, let this, my retreat, be perfect, in you, for you, through you. Amen.

What then, my Lord Jesus, was your public life?

[*Jesus speaks:*] "I tried to save men by word and by works of mercy. Before, in my life at Nazareth, I was content to save them by prayer and penance. Now I show my zeal for souls publicly. But though my life became more active it was always partly solitary and was always a life of prayer and penance and interior recollection. Often I went into the solitude apart, at night or for days together, to pray alone. Except for the time devoted to preaching the Gospel, mine was a life of solitude. It was a life of fatigue, long journeys, and long sermons; days in the desert without shelter or shade cannot be without fatigue and physical suffering, intemperate weather, nights without shelter, uncertainty, nourishment snatched when work permitted; all these mean suffering. Then there was *moral* suffering: men's in-

gratitude, their deaf ears, their ill will, their hard hearts, my healing hand laid daily on all sorts of sufferings of the human body. Souls saved, so many lost to be found, such human suffering, that of the righteous, that of my Mother, the vision ever growing nearer and greater of my Passion; of enmities as the only response to my words of salvation, to my words of love offered to all men; above all, the ingratitude of that 'faithless and perverse generation' wounding my tender compassionate Heart."
— Retreat at Nazareth, November 1897, MH 48–49

Jesus in the Holy Eucharist

Lord Jesus, you are in the Holy Eucharist. You are there, a yard away in the tabernacle. Your body, your soul, your human nature, your divinity, your whole being is there, in its twofold nature. How close you are, my God, my Savior, my Jesus, my Brother, my Spouse, my Beloved!

You were not nearer to the Blessed Virgin during the nine months she carried you in her womb than you are to me when you rest on my tongue at Holy Communion. You were not closer to the Blessed Virgin and St. Joseph in the caves at Bethlehem or the house at Nazareth or during the flight into Egypt, or at any moment of that divine family life than you are to me at this moment and so many others — in the tabernacle. St. Mary Magdalene was no closer to you when she sat at your feet at Bethany than I am here at the foot of this altar. You were no nearer to your apostles when you were sitting in the midst of them than you are to me now, my God. How blessed I am!

It is wonderful, my Lord, to be alone in my cell and converse there with you in the silence of the night — and you are there as God, and by your grace. But to stay in my cell when

I could be before the Blessed Sacrament — why, it would be as though St. Mary Magdalene had left you on your own when you were at Bethany to go and think about you alone in her room! It is a precious and devout thing, O God, to go and kiss the places you made holy during your life on earth — the stones of Gethsemane and Calvary, the ground along the Way of Sorrows, the waves of the sea of Galilee — but to prefer it to your tabernacle would be to desert the Jesus living beside me, to leave him alone, going away alone to venerate the dead stones in places where he is no longer. It would be to leave the room he is in — and with it his divine companionship — to go to kiss the floor of a room he was in, but is in no longer. To leave the tabernacle to go and venerate statues would be to leave the Jesus living at my side to go into another room to greet his portrait.

Is it not true that someone in love feels that he has made perfect use of all the time he spends in the presence of his beloved? Apart from them, is not that time used best which is employed in doing the will or furthering the welfare of his beloved in some other place?

— Retreat at Nazareth, November 1897, SA 98–99

HUMILITY

You said, O my God, "Learn of me, for I am meek and humble of heart," and you give us a true example of humility. You, God, made yourself man, you made yourself the lowest of men, a humble workman in that little Nazareth where I have lived, and when you passed from the hidden life to your public life what humility you showed in your words and acts, in your teaching and your example. When you work miracles you command that nothing should be said of them, that

no one should be told when you let your apostles see your
glory — you tell them to be silent until your Resurrection.
When you are called to a sick man you go at once. When
anyone asks you for something you do it at once. When
you are persecuted you flee. In nothing do you show yourself to be God, King, All Powerful. When you are roughly
spoken to you answer gently. When you are driven out you
depart without speaking. When you are refused hospitality
you go elsewhere. Everywhere you humble yourself, and in
your teaching it is the same. "Woe to the rich, it is more
difficult for them to enter into heaven than for a camel to
pass through the eye of a needle." "The Son of Man is meek
and humble of heart." "Unless you become like little children you shall not enter the kingdom of heaven." "He who
exalts himself shall be humbled, and he that humbles himself
shall be exalted." "All pride is an abomination before God."
"Do not let yourselves be called Master." "Take the lowest
place." "He shall be the greatest among you who makes himself the lowest and the servant of all." "I hold myself among
you as one who serves." "I wash your feet that you may do
the same for one another." "If anyone gives you a blow upon
one cheek turn the other to him." "If anyone asks for your
cloak give him your coat also." "Resist not evil." "I do not
seek the glory of men."

My God, you have always so taught humility by word and
example that you have made it one of your chief character-
istics. You who were so great, teach me, who am so small
and mean, to be humble like you. Your humility was to be
an example for all men. You so comprehended the difference
between the Creator and his creatures that you wished your
human nature (though it made up one Person with your divine nature) to render the homage of an infinite humility to
the Divinity, whose infinite grandeur you were able clearly to

comprehend. So, if you chose to be humble, how much more should I be humble; I, for whom St. Augustine said "Humility is the truth," should look upon myself as nothing, as a worm. Worse in some respects than the fallen spirits, not in all respects, but in that of having abused your grace and in having sinned innumerable times after having received your pardon.

For me indeed "Humility is the truth." Truth is for me to despise myself. Truth for me, who falls every day, every hour, is to think meanly of myself, of the baseness of my past and my present life, of the mean prompting of my spirit. I, who have so often deceived myself, must think of the weakness of my virtue which every day I see fail before the smallest temptation. I must be *humble in thought,* knowing myself and facing my own misery, past and present, the faults that I have, the virtues that I have not, the infirmities that I have, and the natural gifts that I do not possess. I *must be humble in my desires,* without any ambition, or any wish for man's esteem, but desire on the contrary that they should know the truth and take me at my real value as a worm, as something proud, cowardly, obstinate, and ungrateful. I must not indulge in day dreams (it is a waste of time), especially in evil imaginations full of vanity and worldliness, inspired by ambition; I must be afraid of myself, afraid of my own judgment and integrity and courage. I must attribute to God only whatever good there may be in me, and to myself alone the evil I do.

Humble in speech. I must speak little, saying no good of myself, never revealing unless under great necessity, all the graces God gives me; never saying anything which could give a good opinion of myself to others except under necessity. I must hide all that might give a good opinion of myself to others of my natural and supernatural gifts (though none come from myself, but all from God alone). I must hide any good that I may do if God does any through me. "Let not your right hand know what your left hand does." "When you pray shut your door and let God alone see you." I must speak humbly and gently and never give a proud answer to those who speak proudly to me; I must be humble and gentle with great or small whether I am reproached or praised, whether in prosperity or adversity; whether I be flattered or menaced I must be humble in speech and humble in the thought of death.

Humble in actions. I must believe no work beneath me, since Jesus was a carpenter for thirty years, and Joseph all his life. With this example I should, on the contrary, look upon any occupation or work as a great privilege. I must welcome with love and readiness any occasion for humility, any humiliation that emulates the humility of Jesus, and since if my sins were known to men nothing would seem to them bad enough for me, let me avoid all lofty occupations and all high positions because Jesus was lowly and despised. I must accept no promotion whatever it may be, unless obedience imposes it on me and if I see that it is a duty and the will of God.

— Retreat at Nazareth, November 1897, MH 73–76

Manual Labor

O God, inspire me with the knowledge you want me to have regarding manual work.

[*Jesus speaks:*] "In this matter, as in lowliness and poverty, I want from you what I required from myself. Yours is a blessed vocation, my child — how fortunate you are! Just take me as a model: do what you think I did and what I would have done. Do not do what you think I should not have done or would not do. Imitate me.

"Work hard enough to earn your daily bread, but less than ordinary workers. They work to earn as much as possible. You and I work only so as to earn a very frugal diet and the poorest of clothing and lodgings, together with enough to give small sums in alms. We do not work more than this, because our detachment from material things and our love of penance lead us to want only the poorest possible clothing, lodging, and food, and only what is absolutely necessary. We work less than other workers because on the one hand we have fewer material needs and on the other we have greater spiritual needs. We try and keep more time for prayer, mental prayer, and spiritual reading, because that is what life was like in the holy house at Nazareth."

How should I work?

"In constant recollection of me, my child, remembering continually that you are working with me and for me, that I myself, Mary and Joseph, St. Mary Magdalene, and our angels are with you; with them, you should contemplate me continually."

— Retreat at Nazareth, November 1897, SP 68

Poverty

[*Christ speaks:*] "My children, the day is almost over. I have only a few words to say to you. My time is almost fulfilled and this Retreat at Ephraim is nearly over. Tomorrow morning we will go to Galilee, but I have still three things to say to you while we are here together in solitude.

"First, poverty, poverty, poverty. Remember my example and my words about poverty. I was born in a stable and brought up in a poor cottage. My parents were poor and I lived poorly by the labor of my hands until that day when I gave up my time to preaching. Since that day I lived by the alms of the faithful, but would take only that by which I could live as simply as when I was a laborer. I had no possessions in the world nor even a stone to lay my head upon. I chose my companions, the apostles, from among the poor, and preached poverty. Remember my words: 'Blessed are the poor.' 'Woe to the rich.' 'If you would be perfect, sell what you have and give it to the poor.' 'If you do not renounce all, you cannot be my disciples.' 'You cannot serve two masters, and cannot love God and money both together.' 'The poor man Lazarus was carried by angels to Abraham's bosom.' Those who leave all to follow me receive a hundredfold in this world, and in the next Life everlasting. I would not let this day end without repeating again: *Poverty, Poverty, Poverty,* Faith in Prayer...Humility."

— Retreat at Ephraim, November 1897, MH 128–29

•

Whoever acknowledges me before humanity I will acknowledge before my Father in heaven.   (Matt. 10:32)

Let us hope! Our Lord sets a very easy price for our salvation: to acknowledge him, not to deny him in thoughts, words, or deeds...not to blush because of him, not to be ashamed of what he was, of the features of his life: poverty, abjection, work,...not to blush when we live on alms, as he did during his public life; not to be ashamed of what did not shame him: the company of the poor, the outcasts, the sinners; not to blush about what he loves, about his children, about any man whoever he may be; not to be ashamed of his doctrine, of the truths of his religion, not to blush about his bride, the holy Church; not to be ashamed of being his

servant and of wearing his livery; not to blush when living
by his commandments and his counsels that are in such con-
tradiction with the ideas of the world; not to be ashamed to
turn the right cheek when we are struck on the left; not to
blush when we are seen as mad, possessed, importunate, for
the love of him, in imitation of him, if he gives us the great
grace of such a conformity with him. One thing only should
put us to shame: not loving him enough. . . . Let us do this, in
fact: *let us love him and hope* for then he will acknowledge
us in heaven! —1897, Hope 52

•

O my Lord Jesus, here is your divine poverty. How greatly I
need your direction — you loved poverty so much. Already
in the Old Testament you showed your predilection for it.
During your life on earth you made it your faithful companion. You left it as an inheritance to your saints, to all those
ready to follow you, to all those who would be your disciples. You inculcated it by the example of your whole life
and glorified it, beatified it, and declared the necessity of it
in your preaching. You chose poor laborers to be your parents. You were born in a cave used as a stable. You worked
in poverty during your childhood. Your first worshipers were
shepherds. When you were presented in the Temple, the offering made for you was the offering of the poor. You lived
as a poor working man for thirty years in Nazareth, where I
am fortunate enough to live, where I have now the unutterable, the inexpressibly profound happiness of raking manure.
Then, during your public life, you lived on alms among poor
fishermen you had chosen to be your companions. "Without
a stone to put under your head." As you told St. Teresa, at
that time you frequently slept in the open air, for lack of a
roof to shelter under. On Calvary you were stripped of your

clothes, your only possession, and soldiers gambled for them among themselves. You died naked, and you were buried by charity and by strangers. "Blessed are the poor!"

My Lord Jesus, how quickly he makes himself poor who, loving you with all his heart, will not permit himself to be richer than his Beloved. My Lord Jesus, how quickly he becomes poor who, remembering that whatever is done for one of your little ones is done for you and whatever is not done for them is not done for you, relieves all the sufferers who come to his gate. How quickly he becomes poor who accepts *with faith your words:* "If you would be perfect, sell all you have and give it to the poor.... Blessed are the poor, for whoever shall have given up his possessions for my sake, shall receive them back a hundredfold here below, and in heaven shall have eternal life," and so many others like them.

My God, I do not know how it is possible for some souls to see you in poverty and themselves voluntarily remain rich, to imagine themselves so much grander than their Master, their Beloved, and not want to be like him in all things — as far as it is for them to decide — and especially in your humbleness. I do not doubt their love for you, my God, but I think there is something lacking in their love — I, at any rate, could not imagine love without a *longing, a compelling longing,* to imitate, to resemble the Beloved, and especially to share all his life's pains, difficulties, and burdens. To be rich, to live in comfort among my possessions while you were poor, deprived, living in misery under the burden of heavy labor — I just could not do it, O God. I could not love like that. "The servant is not above his master," neither is the bride rich while the Bridegroom is poor — especially when he is voluntarily poor, and perfect as well. St. Teresa, tired of the pressures put on her to accept an income for her convent at Avila, sometimes came close to accepting, but when she returned to her oratory and saw the cross, she fell at its feet and begged Jesus, naked on his cross, to give her the grace never to accept an income and to be as poor as he was. I am judging no one, O God; the others are your servants and my brothers, and I cannot but love them, do good to them, pray for them. But for my own part I cannot understand love that does not seek to imitate and does not feel the need to share every cross.

Besides, the poor man's possessions are so great: he has nothing and loves nothing in this world, and so his soul is free. Nothing is especially important to him. It is of little significance to him whether he is sent to one place or another, for he has nothing anywhere, and wants nothing anywhere. He finds God everywhere, and God is the only one from whom he wants anything. Moreover, if he is loyal, God always gives him what is best for his soul. How free he is! How lightly his spirit mounts up into the heavens! How weightless are his wings! His prayers are little troubled by thoughts of natural things great or small (for little things, even the smallest, are as disturbing as the biggest): how little they distract his prayers! Such things do not exist for him.

This was the point you, blessed Mary Magdalene, had reached at Sainte Baume. [*Foucauld refers to the French legend, of great antiquity, that Mary Magdalene fled persecution in Palestine and settled as an anchoress in Provence.*] And I believe Jesus has given me you to teach me poverty, complete, perfect poverty, not merely "having no more than, and being able to call on no more than, the poorest worker," as I vowed, and as the imitation of Jesus requires. Total poverty is more than this. It is *poverty of Spirit* which you, Lord Jesus, said was blessed, that makes every — absolutely every — material thing a matter of complete indifference, so that we can brush everything aside, break with everything as

St. Mary Magdalene did in the holy cave. This is the poverty that leaves no attachments at all to temporal things, but
completely empties the heart, leaving it whole and entirely
free for God alone. God then refills it with himself, reign-
ing in it alone, filling it wholly with himself, and putting into
it — though not for itself, but for himself, for his own sake —
love for all men, his children.

The heart then knows nothing and holds nothing but these
two loves. Nothing else exists for it any longer, and it lives
on earth as though it were not there, and in continuous contemplation of the only real necessity, the *only Being,* and in
intercession for those whom the Heart of God longs to love.

— Retreat at Nazareth, November 1897, SA 62–65

Lowliness

O my Lord Jesus, graciously permit me to be you in this
meditation. It was you who said: "The servant is not above
his master," and in doing so you commanded me not to be
higher than you in the eyes of men, as far as my life in this
world is concerned. How ought I to practice this lowliness?

[*Jesus answers:*] "Notice first that after I said, 'The servant
is not above his master,' I added, 'It is enough for the servant
if he be as his master.' Thus I do not want you to be above
me, but no more do I want you to be lower than me. If there
are exceptions to this, there is certainly none for you, whom I
have so often called to the vocation of imitating me perfectly
and me alone. Try then to be in the eyes of the world what
I was during my life at Nazareth, neither higher nor lower.
I was a poor working man, living by the labor of my hands:
men took me for unlearned, illiterate. As my parents, near
relatives, cousins, and friends I chose poor laborers like myself, artisans and fishermen. I spoke to them on equal terms;

I dressed like them, lived like them and ate like them while I was with them. Like all poor people, I was exposed to scorn, and it was because in the eyes of the world I was a poor 'Nazarene' that I was so persecuted and ill-treated during my public ministry — that the first time I spoke in the synagogue they called me Beelzebub and in Judea devil and possessed. It was why they treated me as an imposter and traitor and killed me on a gallows between two thieves. They took me for an ambitious nobody.

"Be taken as what I was taken for, my child, unlearned, poor, of lowly birth, also for what you really are: unintelligent, untalented, and ungifted. Always look for the meanest tasks, but cultivate your mind as far as your director bids. But do it secretly. Do not let the world know. I was infinitely wise, but no one knew it. Do not be afraid to study; it is good for your soul. Study zealously to become better, to know me and love me better, to know my will and do it more perfectly, and also to become more like me, who am perfect Knowledge. Be very unlearned in the eyes of men, and very learned in the knowledge of God at the foot of my tabernacle. I was lowly and despised beyond all measure.

"Seek out, ask for, and love those occupations that will humiliate you: piling dung, digging, whatever is lowest and most uncouth. The less important you are in this way, the more like me you will be. If you are thought a fool, so much the better. Give infinite thanks for it to me. They treated me as a madman — it is one of the ways I offer you of being like me. If they throw stones at you, mock you, curse you in the streets, so much the better. Thank me for it: I am giving you an infinite grace — for did they not do as much for me? How fortunate you should think yourself when I give you such close resemblance to me. But do not do anything to merit such treatment — nothing eccentric or strange. I did nothing so as to be treated like that: I did not deserve it — on the contrary. But still they did it to me. Equally, you might do nothing to deserve it, but if I give you the grace of being subjected to it, thank me generously. Do nothing to hinder it, and do not stop it. Endure everything with great joy and gratitude to the Lord that gives it, as though it were a most acceptable present from a brother.

"Do everything as I would have done it and everything I did. Do not do only pleasant things, but devote yourself to the meanest tasks. In everything — your dress, your lodging, the freedom and politeness of your manner to the unimportant — show your level to be that of the lowest. Carefully hide anything that might raise you in your neighbor's eyes. But in my presence, in the silence and solitude of the tabernacle, study and read, for then you are alone with me, my holy parents, and your mother St. Mary Magdalene, and the doors are shut. At my feet, you should expand, doing whatever your director tells you to improve yourself and make yourself more holy — so as to bring greater consolation to my heart."

— Retreat at Nazareth, November 1897, SA 65–67

RESOLUTIONS

In my thoughts, words, and actions, whether directed to myself or my neighbor, I must never trouble about worldly position, celebrity, human esteem, but respect the poor equally with the rich. I must take as much trouble about the humblest workman as about a prince, since God appeared as a humble workman. Always, for myself, seek the lowest place, and be as low as my Master, so as to be with him and walk in his steps like a faithful servant and disciple (since in his

infinite and incomprehensible goodness he lets me speak so),
as a faithful brother, a faithful spouse. Thus I must arrange
my life so that I am the lowest and most despised of men,
so that I live it beside my Master, my Lord, my Brother, my
Spouse, my God who was the outcast of the people, and the
reproach of the earth, a worm and no man.

It is my desire to live in poverty, abjection, and suffering,
in solitude and neglect, so that all my life I may be beside my
Master, my Brother, my Spouse, my God, who lived thus all
his life, and has given me the example ever since his birth.

—Retreat at Nazareth, November 1897, MH 44–45

•

I must, with Jesus in the manger, embrace humility, poverty,
detachment, abjection, solitude, suffering. I must make little
of human greatness and the respect and approval of men, but
I must respect the poor as much as the rich. For myself I must
always seek the lowest of the low places, and arrange my life
so that I may be the last and the most despised among men.

When I am sad, discouraged about myself and about
others, I must think of Jesus in his glory, sitting on the right
hand of the Father forever, and rejoice. I should at these
times say the glorious mysteries of the Rosary, so as to bathe
my spirit in their joy.

Our Lord speaks. "Never worry about small things. Break
away from all that is small and mean, and try to live on the
heights, not from pride, but from love.

"You must break with all that is not me. Make to yourself
a desert where you will be as much alone with me as Mary
Magdalene was alone in the desert with me. It is through detachment that you will attain to this, by driving out all mean
thoughts, all littlenesses which are not evil in themselves, but
which succeed in scattering your mind far from me, when

you should be contemplating me from morning to night. Fix your mind on me as you work, as you pray; contemplate me unceasingly and give all the time you can to prayer and holy reading, which will unite you to me and through which I will speak to you as I spoke to my parents and to Mary Magdalene at Nazareth and at Bethany. He who loves has his beloved always in his mind; that time is to him well spent that is spent in contemplating him, and that time is to him wasted in which he is out of his sight. He counts as profitable only those hours in which he contemplates the only thing that to him has any reality. All else is for him emptiness and nothingness. Let your soul melt into mine, immerse yourself in me, lose yourself in me. Think of how often I have told you to hope for the day when you will lean forever on my breast. And since I allow it I tell you now to begin to live this sweet life, in silence with Mary Magdalene and my Mother and St. Joseph, lay your head upon my breast and so accomplish your pilgrimage."

I must never lose one chance, one single moment of being in the presence of the Blessed Sacrament, whatever may be the moral or material difficulties, or whatever danger or suffering must be faced in order to do so. The whole world is nothing beside my Master who dwells in the Tabernacle.

I must be humble in thoughts, words, and acts. Never seek the approval of men, but love to be despised by them. He who loves is humble, because he feels small and mean beside his Beloved. He who loves imitates the Beloved, and Jesus was meek and humble of heart.

Humility is the crown of all virtues, and is necessary if we are to please God; pride spoils all.

Ought I to cling to staying at Nazareth? No, not more than to anything else. I should cling to nothing but the will of God. I should feel that it is a great grace to live at Nazareth, be happy in it and be grateful, but I should not attach myself to it. As soon as it is no longer the will of God that I should stay there, I should leave it instantly without hesitation, or a backward look, and go wherever his will calls me.

Our Lord speaks. "One of the reasons for which I made myself poorer than the poorest working man is that I came to teach men to despise honors, that I came to teach men to despise worldly goods, and to give an example of complete poverty and deepest abjection. You have the same reasons as I, for it is part of your vocation to preach the Gospel from the housetops, not by word, but by your life."

—Retreat at Nazareth, November 1897, MH 91–93

Chapter 2

"Cry the Gospel with Your Life"

I see very clearly that God's will is that I should follow him in the closest conformity to his earthly life; I can no longer have any doubt that this is my vocation.
— June 27, 1895

The life of Nazareth can be followed anywhere; follow it in the place where it is most helpful to your neighbors. — May 18, 1905

The following selections reflect the path from Foucauld's experience in the Holy Land to his ultimate destination in the Sahara. Three years in Palestine had convinced him that his imitation of the hidden life of Jesus did not require his literal presence in Nazareth. Nazareth, as he wrote, "is everywhere." But it was the desert of North Africa that particularly beckoned. In part this reflected the gradual recognition that his vocation was not for himself alone. Even during his years as a monk he had begun to conceive of a new type of religious community, a "fraternity" of "Little Brothers of Jesus," who would pursue a contemplative life in the midst of the poor.

Foucauld believed that Morocco or Algeria — the back-drop to his earlier adventures as a soldier and explorer,— offered the ideal setting for his plan. The remote austerity of the desert was certainly an attraction. But Foucauld was equally drawn by the opportunity to implant the Gospel in a non-Christian land. He was, at heart, a missionary, inspired by Christ's call to proclaim the Gospel and to "make disciples of all the nations." Yet he departed significantly from traditional methods of mission. Rather than establish big institutions or proclaim the Gospel with words — a fruitless endeavor among the devout Muslims — he aspired to evangelize according to the model of Jesus during his hidden years in Nazareth: through dialogue, friendship, and living witness. The best witness to the Gospel, he believed, was a holy life.

THE SEARCH FOR A VOCATION

God calls all the souls he has created to love him with their whole being, here and thereafter, which means that he calls all of them to holiness, to perfection, to a close following of him and obedience to his will. But he does not ask all souls to show their love by the same works, to climb to heaven by the same ladder, to achieve goodness in the same way. What sort of work, then must *I* do? Which is *my* road to heaven? In what kind of life am *I* to sanctify myself? Apart from the universal calling of all of us to perfect love, to holiness, to the following of Jesus, and obedience to his will in everything, however small, a calling at the last to heaven, what is the particular and special vocation that he puts before me and you and each one of us? ...

This question: "What kind of life am I going to undertake?" is the question of *vocation*. And it has got to be answered rightly. For if it is answered rightly and we take the way to which God calls us we shall be living obediently to him, we shall be strengthened by his help, and so we shall come to heaven. But if, on the contrary, the question is answered wrongly, then we shall be living in disobedience to God; we shall not be on the road that he has mapped out for us, we shall be without the helps that he has prepared for that road, and it will be very difficult to get to heaven. This shows how extremely important it is not to make a mistake in this matter of vocation: if we allow ourselves to be deceived about it we shall be in the state of disobeying God....

This vocation is God's call to undertake such-and-such a sort of holy life in preference to all others, his urgent call to each individual soul to sanctify itself in this particular way. There can never be any question of *choosing* a vocation: the word "choice" is excluded by the word "vocation," which means "calling," a call from God. Therefore we do not "choose a vocation" but seek to find *our* vocation, to do all we can to hear the divine Voice calling us, to make sure what he is saying — and then to obey him. Where vocation is concerned God speaks, calls, commands: man has not to choose but to listen and obey.   — 1903, Sermons 70–71

From a Letter to Abbé Huvelin, November 22, 1893, Expressing Reservations about the Trappist Life

By the command of the Holy Father, some very good changes have been made in our order.... But we are turning ever more completely and further away from the poverty and the humility of the lowly life of Nazareth that I came here to seek, and from which I am infinitely far from being deterred — a life I am deeply troubled to see Our Lord living alone, without a single soul or a single group in the Church today dreaming of living it with him, and sharing, for love of him and in his love, in the blessedness of the most holy Virgin and St. Joseph.

Is there no way of forming a little congregation to lead that life, living solely by the labor of its own hands — as did Our Lord, who supported himself neither by alms nor offerings? Would it be impossible to find a few souls ready to follow Our Lord in this — to follow him by following *all* his precepts, totally renouncing all property, collective no less than individual, and thus putting aside what Our Lord himself rejected — all legal matters, conflicts, and troubles, making an absolute duty of almsgiving — when they have two coats, giving one away, when they have food, giving to those who have none, keeping nothing back for the morrow; following all the examples set by his hidden life and all the precepts uttered by his lips? A life of work and prayer, not with two kinds of religious, as there are in Citeaux, but one, as St. Benedict wanted — but not using St. Benedict's complicated liturgy, but long hours of prayer, the rosary, the holy Mass. Our liturgy closes the doors of our monasteries to Arabs, Turks, Armenians, and so on, who are good Catholics but do not know a word of our languages. I so long to see such small "nests" of men living an ardent and hardworking life, reproducing Our Lord's own, established under his protection and under the guardianship of Mary and Joseph, close to all the mission stations of the East, now so isolated, so that they could offer refuge to the souls of the peoples of these countries called by God to serve him and love him alone.

Is it a dream, Monsieur l'Abbé — a diabolical illusion? Or is it an idea, or an invitation, sent from God?   — SA 28–29

From a Letter to Abbé Huvelin, October 22, 1898

What I secretly dream of, without confessing or admitting it
even to myself, even indeed, trying to expel it, for it is constantly recurring (and I am admitting it to you because you
ought to know the lowest depths of my soul), what I invol-
untarily dream of is something very simple and numerically
small, resembling the simple communities of the Church's
early days. A few souls united to lead the life of Nazareth,
living like the Holy Family by their own labor and practicing
the Nazarene virtues in contemplating Jesus — a little family,
a little *monastic* home, quite small and simple, and certainly
not Benedictine. . . .

If later Our Lord chooses to send me a few souls to live
the life of Nazareth in one of the deserts of the Holy Land
where he walked and preached the Gospel in former times,
to live with the contemplation, work, hospitality, charity, and
simplicity of the primitive ages, I am ready to obey. I should
equally be following Our Lord; crosses and conflict would
replace the worker's obscurity — as they did for him; there
would be less complete withdrawal, but more acts of charity.
I am in your hands, wanting only one thing, to glorify our
beloved Jesus as much as I can. Do for your child what in the
light of his presence seems to you most pleasing to his Heart.

—SA 120–21

•

We wish to found on the Moroccan frontier, not a Trappist
monastery, not a big, rich monastery, not a money-making
farm, but a small, humble hermitage where a few poor
monks live on a little fruit and barley harvested with their
own hands. They would live in a small, narrow enclosure
in the penitence and adoration of the Holy Sacrament, never

leaving and never preaching, but giving hospitality to anyone who comes, good or bad, friend or enemy, Moslem or Christian. This is Evangelism not by talk, but by the presence of the Very Holy Sacrament and the offer of the Divine Sacrifice, prayer, penitence, the practice of Evangelical virtues, charity — a charity that is fraternal and universal, sharing the last crust of bread with every pauper, every guest, every stranger who comes, and receiving every human being as a beloved brother.   — June 23, 1901, Witness 75

Reflections from Béni-Abbès, December 1902

I am in the house of Nazareth with Mary and Joseph, like a younger brother sitting opposite my elder brother Jesus, who is here night and day in the Sacred Host. I must behave toward my neighbor in a way fitting to this place, this company, as I have seen Jesus do, setting me an example. In the "Fraternity" [*Foucauld's name for his hermitage and its intended community*] I must always be humble, gentle, and ready to serve as were Jesus, Mary, and Joseph at the holy house at Nazareth. To serve others, I need gentleness, humility, abjection, and charity.

In every sick person I should see, not a human being, but Jesus, and so should show him respect, love, compassion, joy, and gratitude at being able to serve him, zeal and gentleness. I should serve the sick as I do the poor, making myself do the lowliest services for them all, as Jesus washed the apostles' feet.

I must tolerate the presence of evil people, as long as their wickedness is not corrupting others — as Jesus tolerated Judas. Resist not evil. I must accede to requests, even unjust ones, out of obedience toward God and so as to do good to souls by humbling myself in this way, treating others as God

did. I must continue to do good for the ungrateful, in imitation of God who makes rain fall on the just and unjust alike.
"If you show goodness only toward the good, what merit is
there?" "Show goodness toward the wicked and ungrateful
and hostile, as did God himself." Every living human being,
however wicked, is a child of God, an image of God and
a member of Christ's body: there must therefore be respect,
love, attention, and solicitude for their physical relief, and an
extreme zeal for the spiritual perfection of every one of them.

I must want to suffer cold, heat, or anything else, liking it,
enjoying it, so as to have a bigger sacrifice to offer to God
and be more closely united with Jesus. I shall thus be able to
glorify him better by offering him a superabundant tribute of
sufferings and receive both on earth and in heaven a deeper
knowledge and love of Jesus. The less of everything we have,
the more like the crucified Jesus we are — the more devoted
to the cross we are, the greater glory we give Jesus who is
nailed there. Every cross is profitable, for every cross makes
us one with Jesus.

I should have nothing more or better than Jesus of Nazareth had it. I should rejoice and long to have less rather
than more.

At every moment, I *should live today as though faced with
the prospect of dying this evening as a martyr.*

"One thing is necessary": to do at all times what would
be most pleasing to Jesus, to be continually ready for martyrdom and accept it *without a shadow of a defense,* as did the
divine Lamb, doing so in Jesus, through Jesus, and for Jesus.

I should rejoice not in what I have but in what I lack,
in lack of success and in penury, for then I have the cross
and poverty of Jesus, the most precious possession the earth
can give.

Abjection: service to others. I must decide on a definite

number of very lowly daily tasks and do them, as Jesus came to Nazareth "to serve." —SA 145–48

•

What I think it might be best to do for the conversion of Morocco is organize a little legion of religious, dedicated both to contemplation and good works, living in great poverty by manual labor. Its simple rule might be summed up in three phrases: perpetual adoration of the Blessed Sacrament exposed, limitation of the hidden life of Jesus at Nazareth, and life in mission countries. Such a little legion would be a vanguard ready to throw itself into the field of Morocco and dig there, at the feet of the Sacred Victim and in the Name of the Sacred Heart of Jesus, a first trench into which the preaching missionaries would then throw themselves as soon as possible afterward. With this purpose in mind, and with the encouragement of my holy and beloved bishop, Mgr. Bonnet, bishop of Viviers, I asked and obtained permission from the right reverend apostolic prefect of the French Sahara to establish myself at a point in his prefecture close to the Moroccan frontier. —January 1903, SA 145–46

From a Letter of April 8, 1905

I am an old sinner who since almost immediately after his conversion, nearly twenty years ago, has been powerfully drawn by Jesus to lead his life at Nazareth. Since that time I have been struggling to imitate him — though, alas, very poorly — and I spent several years in dear, blessed Nazareth as servant and sacristan to a convent of Poor Clares. The only reason why I left that blessed place five years ago was to receive holy orders. I am now an unattached priest of the diocese of Viviers, my final retreats before ordination to the

diaconate and priesthood having shown me that the life of
Nazareth, which was my vocation, ought to be led not in the
Holy Land I love so much, but among the most distressed
souls, the sheep most completely lost. The divine feast of
which I am the minister must be offered not to the brethren
and their relations and the rich neighbors, but to the lamest
and blindest of men, the most abandoned souls, those without priests. When I was young, I traveled through Algeria
and Morocco. Morocco is as big as France and has ten mil-
lion inhabitants, but there is not a single priest in the interior.
In the Algerian Sahara, which is seven or eight times the size
of France and with a population greater than was formerly
thought, there are a dozen missionaries. It seemed to me that
there was no more abandoned race than these, and I asked
and obtained the permission of the Most Reverend Apostolic
Prefect of the Sahara to settle in the Algerian Sahara and lead
there either alone or with a few priests or laymen, brothers
in Jesus, a life as close as possible to the hidden life of our
beloved Jesus at Nazareth.   —SA 137–38

MISSION

A Meditation Written in 1897

[*Jesus speaks:*] "*Your vocation:* Preach the Gospel silently as
I did in my hidden life, and as also did Mary and Joseph.

"*Your rule:* Follow me, Do what I did, In every situation ask yourself: What would Our Lord have done? Then
do that. That is your only rule, but it is absolutely binding
on you.

"*Your mind:* It should be full of the love of God, forgetful
of yourself. It should be full of the contemplation and joy of

my beatitude, of compassion and sorrow for my sufferings, and of joy at my joys. It should be full of suffering for the sins committed against me and an ardent longing to glorify me. It should be a mind full of love for your neighbor for my sake, for I love all men as a father loves his children. It should be full of longing for the spiritual and material good of all men for my sake. It should be a mind free, tranquil, at peace. Everything in it should be there for God's sake alone; nothing for your own sake, or for the sake of any creature.

"Your interior prayer: First method: 1. What do you want to say to me, O God? 2. For my own part, this is what I want to tell you — 3. Saying nothing else, gaze on the Beloved. — Second Method: *Quis? Quid? Ubi? Quibus auxiis? Cur? Quomodo? Quando?* [Who took part in the incident? What did they do? Where was it? Who else was present? Why? In what way did things happen? When?]

"Attendance at Mass: Divide it into three parts: 1. Up to the consecration: offer me and offer yourself to my Father and bring your intentions before him. Give thanks to me for my cross, asking my forgiveness for having made it necessary. 2. From the consecration to the Communion: adore me on the altar. 3. After the Communion: adore me in your heart, give thanks to me, love me, rejoice, be silent.

"Thinking about death: Remember that you ought to die as a martyr, stripped of everything, stretched naked on the ground, unrecognizable, covered with wounds and blood, killed violently and painfully — and desire that it be to-day. That I may grant you this infinite grace, watch loyally, carry your cross faithfully. Remember that your death must inevitably flow out of your life — and on that account, realize the insignificance of a great many things. Think often of death, so as to prepare for it and appraise things at their true value." —SA 49–50

Writing in Nazareth

[*St. John the Baptist speaks:*] "You have all his hidden life. He made it for you with his own hands, out of nothing, so perfectly that you cannot change it without diminishing this divine conformity, so perfect, that whatever you may do, you cannot increase this blessed resemblance; it is enough for you to maintain everything in its present state.

"Fall on your knees, give thanks, adore, bless, weep tears of gratitude, weep with emotion and gratitude, lose yourself in amazed thankfulness, repeat a thousand times over: *Misericordias Domini in aeternum cantabo,* lose yourself in remorsefulness, thanksgiving, and infinite blessings . . . and be careful not to undo what God has done . . . to separate what God has joined. "He who will persevere to the end shall be saved." Persevere! Persevere! Jesus persevered for thirty years in this life, I persevered for thirty years in the desert. Persevere!

"I don't tell you that Jesus will always leave you in this life; that is his secret; but you, you should live at all times without wishing for a different one, without thinking of a different one, without preparing yourself for a different one (unless God orders you to do so through his representative), until God either calls you to him from Nazareth, as he did with our father St. Joseph who is present among us, or calls you to the desert as he did with your brother Jesus, or calls you to public life, as he has also done for your brother Jesus and me.

"In your heart of hearts don't attach yourself to any of these three ways of life more than to the two others, since all three are equally perfect. Be equally ready to take up at the slightest word from God the one among the three which he wishes."   —Carrouges 285

•

[*Our Lord speaks:*] "One of the reasons why I wanted to be poorer than the poorest worker was because I came to teach men to despise honors, to despise this world's goods, and because I wanted to give them an example of the most extreme poverty and the most profound abasement. Do the same thing. Your reasons will be the same as mine, with one last one: it is part of your vocation to proclaim the Gospel from the rooftops, not by what you say, but by how you live." — Retreat at Nazareth, November 1897, SA 57

•

You want to know what I can do for the natives. If we started speaking to them about Our Lord, they would surely flee. We must first get their confidence, make friends with them, do small things for them, give them good advice; out of friendship with them, we can discreetly get them to follow *the natural religion*, proving to them that Christians love them. — October 23, 1905, Witness 141

•

Does my presence do any good here? Contact with the natives helps to lessen the feeling of strangeness, tames them, and slowly makes taboos and prejudices disappear. It is very slow, a very little thing. It is painful to see the reign of evil all around, the lack of good, the enemies of the Lord who are so enterprising, the friends who are so faltering, and to see oneself so miserable after so many blessings. However, one should not be sad but should look above it all, to our Beloved Lord. For it is he whom we love and not ourselves, and it is his good that concerns us. Hope is a duty — charity hopes for all — hope is but faith in the goodness of God.

He is good and all-powerful. Unquestionably, he leaves us free, and often we use our freedom lamentably, but while leaving us free, he still remains the master and can at his will send a grace so powerful that it overwhelms everything, transforms everything. He has already done enough for us to make us believe in his love. For the Sahara, which is eight or ten times the size of France and which, without being heavily populated, is inhabited everywhere, there are only twelve or fifteen priests, all at El-Goléa or at Ouargla. There are difficulties of all kinds and on all sides.

—November 18, 1907, Witness 158

•

[Jesus'] methods in the cradle, at Nazareth, and on the cross were: Poverty, Abjection, Humiliation, Abandonment, Persecution, Suffering, Crucifixion. These are our arms, those of our Divine Spouse who asks us to let him continue his life in us, he who is the only Lover, the only Spouse, the only Savior, and also the only Wisdom and the only Truth. We will find none better than he, and he has never aged. Let us follow this "unique model" and we shall be certain of accomplishing much good, for thenceforth it will not be we who are living, but he who lives in us. Our acts are no longer our own, human and miserable, but his, divinely effective.

—January 15, 1908, Witness 164

•

The fundamental virtues — Charity, Humility, Gentleness — are missing or they are too weak. Charity is the foundation of our religion. It asks each Christian to love his neighbor as if he were himself. Consequently, the salvation of one's neighbor is as important as the salvation of one's self. *Every*

Christian must be an apostle. That is not advice; it is a command — the command of charity.

All force must be abandoned; we must banish militant ideas from ourselves. Jesus taught us to go "like sheep in the midst of wolves," not to speak with bitterness and unkindness, not with arms.

We must read and reread the Gospel without stopping, so that we will have the spirit, deeds, words, and thoughts of Jesus before us so that we may one day think, talk, and act as he did.   — January 1909, Witness 233

•

Let us return to the Gospel. If we do not abide by it, Jesus will not live in us. Let us return to poverty and Christian simplicity. During nineteen days in France, what struck me most was that all classes of society — above all the least wealthy class and also the Christian families — have increased their tastes for costly and useless things. Carefree, worldly, and frivolous distractions are out of place in such grave times, in times of persecution, and they are not in accord with a Christian life. *The danger lies within ourselves,* and not within our enemies. Our enemies can only lead us to victory. The bad we receive is from ourselves. Return to the Gospel — that is the salvation.   — June 30, 1909, Witness 175

•

My apostolate must be one of goodness. I must make people say this when they see me: "This man is so good that his religion must be good." If someone asks me why I am gentle and good, I must reply, "Because I serve One who is much better than I am. If only you knew how good my Master, Jesus, is." I want to be so good that people will say, "If that is the servant, how, then, is the Master?"

The priest is a monstrance. His role is to show Jesus. He must disappear and make Jesus seen. I must leave a good impression on all who come to see me. I must be everything to everyone. I must laugh with those who laugh, cry with those who cry to lead them all to Jesus.

—December 1909, Witness 174

•

Since my return here, my life is filled with praying and receiving my neighbors. I must see all my poor neighbors. They are becoming my old friends, for I am in my seventh year at Tamanrasset. The sweetness of solitude — I have known it most of my life. Even before I became a Christian, I loved solitude with nature and books, where the world is invisible and sweet. In solitude one is never alone. The spirit was not made for noise, but for taking things in. Life is a preparation for heaven, not only through deserving work, but by the peace and communion with God. But mankind throws itself into infinite discussions. The little good he finds in noise should prove how far he has strayed from his vocation.

—Christmas 1912, Witness 202

•

We must react by simplicity and moderation in our own lives in hope that we will be an example for those around us. By Christian fraternity we must fill the chasm that is created by the differences in conditions. I don't think we should talk much or write much, but we must reform ourselves...we must try to reform those whom we influence...try to spread reform. We must work continuously, without becoming discouraged, against ourselves, the world, and the Devil until the end of time. Act, pray, and suffer — these are our methods.   —July 1914, Witness 234

•

There is always work to be done by example, goodness, and prayer. We can enter into closer relationships with souls that are lukewarm or estranged from the faith, so as to lead them gradually, by the power of our patience, gentleness, and goodness, by the influence of virtue rather than advice, back to a more Christian life or to the faith itself. By entering into friendly relationships with people totally opposed to religion we can, by our goodness and virtue, destroy their prejudices and bring them completely to God. We should enlarge our acquaintanceship both with good Christians, so as to be sustained in the fiery love of God, and with nonpracticing Christians, seeking to establish with them not worldly social relations, but the bonds of cordial friendship, so as to lead them to esteem and trust us, and thus to reconcile them with our faith. One has to be as much a missionary in France as in a country of unbelievers, and being so is the duty of us all, priests and lay people, men and women.

—July 24, 1914, SA 190

•

Be kind and compassionate, and do not be insensitive to any misery. See Jesus in all people. Do unto others as you would have others do unto you.

In light of the love and the virtue of the saints, we must humiliate ourselves and convert ourselves: what they have done we can do. God has never forsaken man.

At every opportunity, enlighten your neighbor and bring good to him.

Be firm but gentle, and keep severity for yourself.

Be prepared to sacrifice all to help your neighbor: "What you do unto one of these children, ye have done unto me."

One does good in haste, for charity is urgent.

Respect our most humble brothers, for they merit it. Treat them as favorites of Jesus, for they are the most simple and pure, and they are without vanity. Let us mix with them as God wishes, being one with them and doing good for their bodies and souls.   —February 5, 1916, Witness 266

•

Think of others and pray for them. Devote yourself to the salvation of others by the means in your power: by praying, being good, and setting an example. When you give alms to the poor, it is to the Creator that you have given. When one puts goodness into the heart of a sinner, it is Purity that one has created. God wished it so, thus making charity to one's neighbor a second duty, "alike unto the first" duty, which is the love of God. There is nothing from the Gospel that has impressed me more or had a bigger effect on my life than this: "As long as you did it to one of these my least brethren, you did it to me." When one remembers that those words came from the mouth of the One Who said, "This is My Body, this is My Blood,..." one is sent with great force to seek Jesus and to love him in "these children," these "sinners," these "beggars," and to use all spiritual means to convert souls and all material means to relieve human misery.
                                    —August 1, 1916, Witness 267

UNIVERSAL BROTHER

From a Prospective Rule for the Little Brothers of Jesus

1. To reproduce as faithfully as possible the life of Our Lord, Jesus Christ of Nazareth, because the greatest perfec-

tion and the greatest love of Our Lord is to be expressed in imitating Our Master, so well loved.

2. To follow this life in Christian countries, Moslem countries, or in other countries with love for Our Lord in the hope of giving our blood in his Name; to follow this life with a love for mankind in the hope that our presence and our prayers and, above all, that the Holy Sacraments will bring good to these unfortunate brothers.

We wish to reproduce the hidden life of Our Lord as St. Francis of Assisi reproduced his public life.

Our lives are divided between prayer and work, the former taking precedence over the latter.

We cannot dream of reciting the Holy Office in European languages to the children, the ignorant, the illiterate, or to foreigners. It will be replaced by the adoration of the Holy Sacraments, prayers, the saying of the Holy Rosary. We will pray morning and night in front of the Holy Sacrament; the days will be consecrated to work.

The conversion of men: each morning and each night there will be a half-hour prayer to ask God to save all men whom Our Lord had so ardently asked him to save during his life.

One of the fundamental points of the congregation is that, following the example of Our Lord of Nazareth, it must support itself by manual labor.

It is forbidden to receive any gift, big or small, for any reason whatsoever — not even for Masses or offerings for prayers or for distribution to the poor. Absolutely nothing must be accepted — not money, not provisions. We will live solely by the work of our hands. In order to be charitable and to help the poor, we will keep no money from one week to the next. On Saturday, when the weekly pay is received, all money that is left over from the week before will be given to the poor. The same applies to provisions. Nothing will be kept from one week until the next.

How will the work be done? We will follow the practices of the poorest people in the poorest country. The work should be easy to do for everyone alike — the educated and ignorant, the strong and weak *alike* would be able to do it.

We will have nothing. We will be like workers for a proprietor.

Each "Nazareth" will be composed of ten to eighteen brothers. Men of letters, illiterates, old, young, priests, and laymen will be received equally.

No distinctions will be made between the fathers and the brothers, or converts. Everyone will be equal and everyone will be called "Brother."

The superior will be called "Brother Servant"; he must be educated, but he need not receive orders.

Following the example of Our Lord, we will be established in villages — in towns of heathen countries throughout — but where there are already missionaries, in villages such as Nazareth, we will be in the outskirts where the land is cheaper and where the poorer people live.

The house will be built like the poorest of the country, with rough stones or planks or twigs interlaced — like the poorest of the region. That is the only Rule.

Around the house, there will be a little garden. Each house and its little enclosure will not be bought, but rented.

If one of the brothers is sent on a voyage, he will travel in the lowest class as the poorest of the poor. He will walk where the poorest walk. If he goes by public transportation — trains or boats — he will travel in the manner of the poor; he will always take the lowest class, the last place in the manner of Our Lord or of the Holy Virgin or St. Joseph.

The poor and the others will always pass in front of the brothers and the sick will pass before the healthy....

All of our efforts will be dedicated to have within us and to show unto others charity, compassion, tenderness, and the infinite goodness of our divine Master.

—June 1896, Witness 51–53

•

That you may be children of your heavenly Father.
(Matt. 5:45)

Here is another word in which we must have true, deep, practical faith.... *We* are all children of God: we must therefore see the beloved children of God in all people, and not just in the good, not just in the Christians, not just in the saints, but in *all* the people. They are all children of God and consequently we must show for all of them, in our thoughts, words, and actions, the tender, affectionate, loving behavior that a brother shows for his brother, behavior that always remains loving, even if the brother sins, commits evil, or misbehaves. Such genuine fraternity among all people, all children of God, leads to tenderness in feelings, sweetness in words, and charity in actions that explain all the precepts of the Gospel concerning charity, peace, and sweetness. Nothing is more natural than these precepts if all people are considered brothers and sisters, the children of the same Father. May we therefore have *faith* in our fraternity with all people.   —1897, Faith 52–53

*From a Rule of the Little Brothers of the Sacred Heart
(1901)*

"You have only one Father, who is in heaven." "God created man in his image." "Whatever you do to the least of these, you do it to me." These three verses are enough to show the Little Brothers their duty of immense charity extended without exception to all men, who are all "children of God," "in the image of God," and "members of Jesus." Faithful to their name and to the heart and cross they wear on their habit as a symbol of infinite Love, and to their divine model, they will carry all men in their hearts as did their Brother and Bridegroom Jesus, who died for the whole human race.

With any soul they meet, they will keep ever before their eyes their mission toward every person. This mission is to bring salvation. In every person, good or bad, friend or enemy, benefactor or persecutor, Christian or unbeliever, they will see a soul to be saved. They will make themselves "all things to all men, in order to gain them all." They will hate evil, but this hatred will never keep them from loving people. They will carry everyone in their hearts, even the most wicked, taking Jesus' heart for their model; they will be friends to one and all in order to be saviors to one and all. Disciples, imitators, and members of Jesus, their life has the same goal as his, to save all men for God's sake. Their life must, like his, be summed up and expressed in one word: Jesus, "savior." They will not bring salvation by preaching but by the offering of the Holy Sacrifice and the presence of the Eucharist. They will bring salvation by practicing virtue, by penance and prayer, and by a charity that sees in every human being only a member of Jesus to lavish with favors and lead to heaven. This is the immense and all-embracing charity that must shine out from the Fraternity as it shone from the Sacred Heart of Jesus.

To make Jesus and charity reign: this is the mission of the Little Brothers of the Sacred Heart of Jesus, as their name says. They must make Jesus and his charity reign in their hearts and around them. Their Fraternities, consecrated to

the Sacred Heart of Jesus, must as he did shine out on earth
and kindle fire there. "I have come to light a fire on earth,
and what will I but that it be kindled?" Everyone far and
wide around us must understand the meaning of our name
and the heart they see on our habits. Everyone must regard
our Fraternities as harbors of Love, "the home of the Sacred
Heart of Jesus, of Divine Love shining on earth, of burning
charity, of the Savior of mankind." —CG 99–100

•

I want to accustom all the inhabitants, Christians, Muslims,
Jews, and nonbelievers, to look on me as their brother, the
universal brother. Already they're calling this house "the fraternity" (*khaoua* in Arabic) — about which I'm delighted —
and realizing that the poor have a brother here — not only
the poor, though: all men. —July 19, 1902, SP 43

•

The work to which I have long seen I ought to dedicate my
life is the building up of two little families, one called the
"Little Brothers of the Sacred Heart of Jesus," and the other
the "Little Sisters of the Sacred Heart of Jesus," both with
the same aim: the glorification of God by the imitation of
the hidden life of Jesus, the perpetual adoration of the sacred Host and the conversion of unbelievers. They would
both take the same form: they would be small, enclosed
fraternities with about twenty brothers or sisters, in which,
following the Rule of St. Augustine and special constitutions
(with solemn vows when Holy Church permits), the hidden
life of Jesus of Nazareth will be followed as faithfully as
possible, and the most Blessed Sacrament, exposed day and
night, will be perpetually adored in love, adoration, sacrifice, prayer, manual labor, poverty, abasement, recollection,

and silence. They will be in the most out-of-the-way parts of non-Christian countries, so that Jesus will be brought to the places where he is least known, and search may be made with him for his most lost and abandoned sheep.

Not knowing any more lost, abandoned, deserted country, none more lacking in workers for the Gospel than the Sahara and Morocco, I have asked and obtained permission to set up a tabernacle on their frontiers, and bring a few brothers together there in adoration of the sacred Victim. I have been living here for several years up till now, alone — *mea culpa, mea culpa, mea culpa.* Unless the grain of wheat falling to the ground dies, it remains alone; if it dies, it brings forth much fruit. I have not died, so I am alone. Pray for my conversion that, dying, I may bear fruit.

                                        —December 15, 1904, SA 160

•

Jesus has set you up forever in the life of Nazareth. Missionary and solitary lives are only the exception for you as for him: carry them out every time his will indicates it clearly; as soon as it is no longer indicated, return to the life of Nazareth.

Make, whether alone, or with a few brothers, the life of Nazareth your objective, in everything and for everything, in its simplicity and its breadth.... No special clothing — like Jesus in Nazareth; no enclosure — like Jesus in Nazareth; a house not far from an inhabited place, but close to a village — like Jesus in Nazareth; not less than eight hours of work a day (manual or other, as much as possible manual) — like Jesus in Nazareth; no large landholdings, no large dwellings, no great expenses, not even large alms, but the utmost poverty in everything — like Jesus in Nazareth. In other words, in everything: Jesus in Nazareth.

Do not try to organize; prepare the establishment of the Little Brothers of the Sacred Heart of Jesus; alone, live as if you were always to remain alone; if you are two, there, a few, live as if you were never to be many. Pray like Jesus, as much as Jesus, allow, as he did, for a great deal of prayer; also as he did, allow for a great deal of manual work, which is not a time taken away from prayer, but given to prayer. Faithfully say the Breviary and the Rosary every day. Love Jesus with all your heart . . . and your neighbor as yourself for love of him. The life of Nazareth can be lived everywhere: even there in the place most useful for one's neighbor.

—July 22, 1905, Carrouges 227

•

The Little Brothers will not only gladly welcome the guests, the poor, the sick who ask for hospitality; they will invite in those whom they encounter, begging them, kneeling if necessary like Abraham to the angels, not to "pass your servants by" without accepting their hospitality, their attentions, their marks of brotherly love. Everyone in the neighborhood must know that the Fraternity is the house of God where every poor or sick person is always invited, called, wanted, welcomed with joy and gratitude by brothers who love and cherish them and regard their entry as the discovery of a great treasure. They are in fact the greatest treasure of all, Jesus himself: Insofar as you do this to one of the least of these brothers of mine, you do it to me.   —SP 43

Chapter 3

Abandonment to the Will of God

*When one loves one longs to be forever in converse
with him one loves, or at least to be always in his sight.
Prayer is nothing else. This is what prayer is. Intimate
intercourse with the Beloved. You look at him, you tell
him of your love, you are happy at his feet, you tell him
you will live and die there.*   —November 29, 1896

*In his spiritual life, as in all things, Charles de Foucauld
patterned himself after Jesus of Nazareth. This extended
to his style of prayer, his intimacy with God, and his
sense of abandonment to divine providence. The writings selected here reflect a deeply mystical sensibility — a striving
for communion with God in all things and circumstances,
whether joyful or sorrowful. In this fashion he embodied
the injunction to "pray without ceasing," explaining that by
prayer he meant no more than "intimate intercourse with the
Beloved." So intimate was this conversation that often, in his
meditations, he recorded not only his own words but Christ's
"response." Certainly he would have embraced St. Paul's de-
scription of the spiritual life: "Now I live, not I but Christ
lives in me." In that same spirit he could say with Christ,
"Not my will, but thine be done."*

THE BEATITUDES

[*Jesus speaks:*] "Blessed are the poor in spirit — those who reject not only material things, which is the first step, but who also climb higher, emptying their souls completely of every attachment, every liking, every desire, every search of which I am not the object. Such poverty of spirit leaves the soul completely empty, voiding it of love for material things, for one's neighbor and for oneself, expelling everything, absolutely everything, from it, leaving it a completely empty space which can be filled wholly by me. Then I can make divine the love for material things they have expelled from their souls so as to give all the room in them to me. They have expelled all these different loves from their souls, and I occupy them completely, so that they are empty of everything else and full of me. Then, in me and for my sake, they begin to love all these other things again, no longer for the sake of the things themselves, but for mine. Then shall their charity be ordered aright. They love all created things for my sake, loving nothing for its own sake, because they owe all their love to me and should lose themselves in me, possessing nothing, not even love, except through me or for my sake. Blessed are the poor in spirit, who are empty of everything else, but so full of me!

"Blessed are they that hunger — those who hunger for justice, the rule of justice on earth, for my reign on earth, who hunger to see me glorified by every soul, who hunger to see my will perfectly fulfilled by all creatures. You should never be without this great hunger for justice, for seeing my will perfectly fulfilled by both yourself and all mankind, for your own total sanctification and the perfect sanctity of all men. This is the hunger that weighs on my own Heart. Feel it more and more, not for your own sake, or for man's, but for God's sake, for the love of God. You will then be blessed indeed, for you will be in perfect harmony with my own heart.

"Blessed are they that mourn — because they are unhappy, poor, bereaved, sick, suffering in body or soul, tried in whatever way. They are blessed because their sufferings will be effective in expiating their sins, because their sufferings detach them from the world and lift up their gaze to me and attach them to myself. More blessed still are those who mourn their sins. And yet more blessed those who weep for sorrow at not seeing me and at being exiled far from me in this vale of tears. Even more blessed are those who mourn my sufferings, my passion, all the sufferings I endured on earth. And most blessed are those who weep from love alone, who weep because they love me, who weep for no particular reason — not from pain nor yet longing, but merely because when they think of me their whole heart melts and they cannot restrain their tears.

"Blessed are they that are hated and persecuted for my sake — blessed indeed for they are imitating me, sharing my lot. True spouses, they share fully in the lot of their Spouse. Blessed, because is there anything more loving than to suffer with the one you love? Blessed, because they have this double happiness. Suffering with their Beloved and for him. Blessed, because through these very sufferings their love for me will grow, increasing proportionately to their sufferings for my sake — and their growing love will not be transitory, but enduring: it will last through time and into eternity. O blessed are they who suffer persecution with me, whose love is growing continually under persecution! Never reject or fear pains, hatred, and persecution suffered for my sake; on the contrary, accept them with joy, blessing, thanksgiving, gratitude to God and men, thanking me from the bottom of your heart, praying for your enemies and executioners, joining — terrestrial angels — with the holy guardian angels in begging me for their conversion, rejoicing from the depths of your hearts at having been found worthy to undergo suffering and humiliation for love of me. Never forget that this is how I treat all those I love especially fondly. . . .

"And how blessed the end of these sufferings will be! The more you have loved me and suffered for me in this world, the more you have been persecuted for my sake, the clearer will be your vision of me, and the more perfectly you will love me for ever in the next."

— Eight Days in Ephraim, 1898, SA 58–60

•

I was hungry and you gave me food.
(Matt. 25:35)

Our Lord thus gives us the true reason for charity, the most powerful. There are others, too. We must give to obey God's oft repeated command; we must obey to imitate him, he who gives so generously, to imitate Jesus who gave so much; we must give because the love of God forces us to carry the love we have for him over to people, his beloved children; we must give out of kindness, solely to practice and cultivate that virtue which must be loved for itself because it is one of God's attributes, one of the divine graces, one of God's perfections, and consequently God himself.

But the most stirring motive for giving, one that, while any of the others quite suffices, exhorts us above all, is that everything we do for our neighbor we do for Jesus himself. That is enough to change our entire life, guide all our actions, our words, and our thoughts. Everything we do for our neighbor is done for Jesus. What an apostolic spirit that gives us! What a spirit of charity! And hence what a thrust to our prayers, our works, our lives! What a life of poverty, charity, and self-denial! What a thirst for spiritual grace, relief for the soul and body! Now we can understand why we must be "men of courage" (cf. Dan. 10:19).

What horizons open up! It places our entire life, both inner and outer, our prayers as well as our rules for living and relations with people, at the service of our neighbors, primarily at the service of their spiritual good, and secondarily their material good, strictly — absolutely strictly — purely, purely *for the sake of Jesus.* Because according to his Word we must believe with divine faith that *everything we do* to our neighbor, we do to Jesus. It therefore follows that if we want to spend our entire life doing the most good to Jesus, we must use our life to do the most good to our neighbor. O my Lord and my God, help me thoroughly understand this truth! Help me do the utmost good to you at every moment of my life by contributing every moment of my life toward doing the utmost good to my neighbor for your sake. And may I never commit any evil, any offense, any imperfection against you, never committing — either in thought, speech, or action — any offense, any imperfection against my neighbor. And may I do all that *for the sake of you and you alone,* because of your Word. "Whatever you did for one of these least brothers of mine, you did for me" (Matt. 25:40).

— 1897, Faith 26

FAITH

Real faith, faith which inspires all one's actions, faith in the supernatural which strips the world of its mask and reveals God in all things; which abolishes the notion of "impossible," and empties the words "anxiety," "danger," and "fear" of their meaning; which gives life calm, peace, deep joy, like a child holding its mother's hand; which detaches the soul so completely from earthly things by showing up their total lack of importance and their childishness; which bestows such confidence in prayer, the confidence of a child asking its father for something useful; the faith which shows that "apart from doing what is agreeable to God, everything is vanity"…oh, how rare that is!…My God, give me real faith! My God, I believe, help the little faith I have!

— Meditations on the Gospel, SP 23

•

There is one thing further you must do. Sell all you have and give it to the poor. You will have treasure in heaven. Then come and follow me. (Luke 18:22)

My God, make me embrace these words with *faith*. It seems so simple yet it is so difficult, and who acts on it? It must be something perfect since only saints do it. Aside from saints, who considers alms to the poor an investment in heaven? Who, except them, gives with the eagerness inspired by such faith? Oh, how human life would change, how points of view would change, how different deeds would be if this *faith* entered souls. To give alms to the poor surely places one in heaven, changing a transitory and perishable asset into an eternal one! If only we actually believed this! Alas, how far we are from this, even those of us who think of ourselves as religious souls!

Who follows Jesus by taking the same path as he, imitating him in everything, truly seeing him as the path, "following" him as the apostles followed him in the union of souls which "followed" his own, forming and modeling themselves perfectly after his soul, in the union of their external life, going where he wanted to go, sharing his poverty, his abjection, everything he wanted to suffer, being what he wanted to be, "following" him by sharing and imitating everything in his interior and exterior life. Who does this, except the saints? Oh, my God, spread *faith* in your words on earth, give it to me, to those whom I must love even more, give it to all your children. Teach me to have faith in charity by considering it a treasure inscribed in heaven and to follow you by imitating you in everything, by imitating your faithful images.   — 1897, Faith 105

•

Why are ye fearful, O ye of little faith?
(Matt. 8:26)

Complete freedom from fear is one of those things we owe wholly to Our Lord. To be afraid is to do him a double injury. First, it is to forget him, to forget that he is with us, that he loves us and is himself almighty, and second it is to fail to bend to his will. If we shape our will to his, as everything that happens is either willed or allowed by him, we shall find joy in whatever happens, and shall never be disturbed or afraid.

So then, we should have the faith that banishes all fear. Beside us, face to face with us, within us, we have Our Lord Jesus, our God whose love for us is infinite, who is himself almighty, who has told us to seek for the kingdom of God and that everything else will be given us. In that blessed and omnipotent company, we must go straight along the path of the greatest perfection, certain that nothing will happen to us that we cannot use as a source of the greatest good for his glory and the sanctification of ourselves and others, and that everything that happens is either willed or permitted by him,

and that therefore, far from lying under the shadow of fear,
we have only to say, "Whatever happens — God be praised!"
praying that he will arrange everything not in accordance
with our ideas, but for his greater glory. We should never
forget the two axioms: "Jesus is with me" and "Whatever
happens, happens by the will of God."

•

*Be of good heart, my daughter; thy faith hath made thee
whole.*   (Matt. 9:22)

Faith is the virtue most commonly rewarded and praised
by Our Lord. Sometimes, as in the case of St. Mary Magdalene, he praised love, at other times, humility. But such
cases are rare. Almost always it was faith he rewarded and
praised.

Why was this? Doubtless because although faith is not
the highest virtue (charity surpasses it), it is nonetheless the
most important, both because it is the foundation of all the
others, including charity, and because it is the most rare.
How wonderful it is really to have the faith which inspires
the believer's every action. Such faith is supernatural, and
strips the mask from the world and reveals God in everything. It makes nothing impossible; it renders meaningless
such words as "anxiety," "danger," and "fear," so that the
believer goes through life calmly and peacefully, with profound joy — like a child hand in hand with his mother. It
fixes the soul in an attitude of such complete detachment
from all material things that it can clearly perceive their
nothingness and puerility. It gives to prayer the confidence
a child shows in asking its father for something reason-
able. It shows the believer that "apart from doing something
pleasing to God, there is nothing that is not a lie." It puts

everything in a new light, revealing men as images of God, to be loved and venerated as portraits of our Beloved, and to be made the recipients of all possible good, and showing us that every other created thing without exception is there to be used as an aid in getting to heaven, by praising God through it, either by our actively using it or by our definite rejection of it.

It is this faith which, by letting us perceive the splendor of God, lets us see our littleness. It leads us to undertake everything pleasing to God, without hesitation, or self-consciousness, never fearing and never drawing back. What a rare thing such faith is. O God, give it to me! I believe — but make my faith grow. O God, I beseech you in the name of Our Lord Jesus Christ: give me faith and love. Amen.

— Retreat at Nazareth, November 1897, SA 69–70

From Nazareth, to His Sister

July 21, 1899

The events of this life have no importance, nor have material things. They are but dreams at a halting-place on the journey, and they pass like dreams and leave no trace. To see things as they really are we must see them in that great light of Faith which illumines our minds with a light so clear that we see things very differently from those poor worldly souls. The habit of seeing things in the light of Faith lifts us above the mists and the mire of the world. It takes us into another atmosphere, into full sunshine, into a calm serenity, into a luminous peace above the clouds and the wind and the storms, a region without twilight or darkness.

We must live by faith and believe that what, by grace, we hope for, we shall possess in glory. Let us love God who will be our infinite recompense, at all moments of our existence, in time and in Eternity. — MH 143

To His Sister

September 1, 1899

Oh, no! Mary Magdalene was not alone at Sainte Baume. She was no more alone than she was at Bethany. But instead of having God visible before her in a mortal shape, she had him invisible in her soul, but he was no less present. She was seated at his feet here as there. This is my life too, dearest, as much as my weakness, my misery, my meanness, my luke-warmness, my cowardice will allow. Try to make it more and more yours. It will not deter you in your other occupations, nor separate you from others, it will take only a moment of your time; only instead of being alone you will have a Companion in your work and your duties. Now and again lower your eyes to your breast and remain in recollection for a few seconds thinking "You are there, my God, and I love you." It will take you no longer than that, and all that you do will be the better for it, for you will have got help, and such help! By degrees you will develop the habit, and you will end by always feeling this sweet companionship of the God of our hearts. Then there will be no more solitude for you. And we shall be more united than ever, for we shall be leading identically the same life.

We shall pass our time in the same manner with the same dear Companion. We must pray each for the other that we may always keep company with the beloved Guest of our souls.

And let my example teach you that we can never say we shall be happier in one place than another, in some circumstances or others, for the very simple reason that it is God, the almighty Power of our souls, who gives us consolation and joy, where, when, and how he will. In one moment he may destroy our dream of happiness; in an instant he makes "the desert to bloom like a lily," and he turns the "night into a glowing light," as says one of the Psalms.

—MH 144–45

•

The best used hour in our lives is that in which we love Jesus most.

A soul does good, not in proportion to its knowledge or intellect, but to its holiness.

I must embrace all men for God's sake in the same love and the same self-forgetfulness. I must be no more anxious about my own health and life than a tree is about a falling leaf.

We must remember only Jesus, think only of Jesus, counting any loss as a profit insofar as it makes more room in us for thought about and knowledge of Jesus, beside whom everything else is nothing.

"I must keep all my powers for God."

—December 1903, SA 156

PRAYER

And rising very early, going out, he went into a desert place: and there he prayed.   (Mark 1:35)

Let us do what Our Lord did and rise early in the morning, while everything is at rest in silence and darkness, when sleep envelops everything in torpor, in profound quiet. Let us rise and watch with God, lifting our hearts to him, laying our souls at his feet, and at this early hour when intercourse is so secret and so sweet let us fall at his feet and enjoy converse with Our Creator. How good he is to let us come to his feet while all is sleeping. How good he is to allow his poor creatures this intercourse with his Sovereign Majesty, with his ineffable beauty. Our whole soul should rejoice in these happy moments, privileged beyond words, privilege of which neither man, nor angel, nor saint is worthy. Let us every day and all our lives do this of which Our Lord sets us an example and which should be our greatest happiness, divine happiness. Let us rise early in the morning, before daybreak, and, while all else is sleeping in silence and shadow, let us begin both our day and our prayers. Before our working day begins let us pass long hours praying at the feet of Our Lord. Let us not only pray part of the night before the day breaks, but pray alone, forgotten by all in that solitude. If prayer in common is enjoined by him, so is secret and solitary prayer, and in both we have his example. Let us follow both precepts and both examples.

— Meditations on the Gospel, MH 17–18

•

O my God, pardon me, pardon me for my coldness, my cowardliness, my wasted time, my pride, my love of my own will, forgive me my weakness and unfaithfulness, the confusion of my thoughts, my forgetfulness of your presence. Forgive, forgive my sins, all the faults of my life, and particularly those I have fallen into since my conversion: I thank you for your many graces. My Lord and my God, come to my aid, help me on whom you have showered your gifts so that I might be converted, and let me use the gifts that you still offer me so that I may do whatever you ask of me, whatever, in your infinite goodness, you call me to do, I who am so unworthy. Turn my heart toward you, my God, for the sake of Our Lord Jesus Christ. You can "of these stones raise up sons to Abraham." You are all-powerful over your creatures, you can do all things in me. Give me a right mind, give me the wisdom that you promise to all who ask for it. Convert my heart and let me glorify you to the utmost till my last breath and through all Eternity. I ask this in the name of Our Savior Jesus Christ. Amen. Amen. Amen.

— Meditations on the Gospel, MH 28–29

Prayer of Abandonment

This was the last prayer of our Master, our Beloved. May it also be ours. And may it be not only that of our last moment, but also of our every moment:

"Father, I put myself in your hands; Father, I abandon myself to you, I entrust myself to you. Father, do with me as it pleases you. Whatever you do with me, I will thank you for it. Giving thanks for anything, I am ready for anything, I accept anything, give thanks for anything. As long as your will, my God, is done in me, as long as your will is done in all your creatures, in all your children, in all those your heart loves, I ask for nothing else, O God. I put my soul into your hands. I give it to you, O God, with all the love of my heart, because I love you, and because my love requires me to give myself. I put myself unreservedly in your hands. I put myself in your hands with infinite confidence, because you are my Father."

— Retreat at Nazareth, November 1897, SA 95–96

•

In spite of everything, you want me to hope, to hope always that I shall receive enough grace to be converted and attain

glory. What is there in common between heaven and me —
between its perfection and my wretchedness? There is your
Heart, O Lord Jesus. It forms a link between these two so
dissimilar things. There is the love of the Father who so loved
the world he gave his only Son. I *must* always hope, because
you have commanded me to, and because I *must* always believe both in your love, the love you have so firmly promised,
and in your power. Yes indeed, remembering what you have
done for me, I must always have such confidence in your love
that, however ungrateful and unworthy I may seem to myself
to be, I can still have hope in it, still count on it, still remain
convinced that you are ready to accept me as the father accepted his prodigal son — and even more ready — and still
remain convinced too that you will not stop calling me to
your feet, inviting me to come to them and giving me the
means to do so.

    —Retreat at Nazareth, November 1897, SA 72–73

•

[*Jesus speaks:*] "When you pray, you should want all that I
want, and only what I want, in the way I want it, and to the
extent I want it: 'Father, may your will be done!' This is the
prayer you will say forever in heaven.

    "Everything God desires, and consequently, everything
you desire, everything God wills, and consequently, everything you want, are to be found in the words: 'Father, may
your will be done.'

    "Prayer is any converse between the soul and God. Hence
it is that state in which the soul looks wordlessly on God,
solely occupied with contemplating him, telling him with
looks that it loves him, while uttering no words, even in
thought."

    —Retreat at Nazareth, November 1897, SA 73–74

•

My children: in prayer, do what I would have you do —
love, love, love.

[*Jesus speaks:*] "Besides the time you should devote every
day solely to prayer, you should lift up your soul toward me
as often as possible throughout the rest of the day. Depend-
ing on the nature of your work you may be able to do so by
thinking continually of me (as is possible in certain manual
occupations), or you may only be able to lift up your eyes
toward me from time to time. At least, let it be as frequently
as possible. It would be very wonderful and very right to be
able to contemplate me unceasingly, never losing sight of me.
But in this world that is not possible for ordinary people; you
will be able to do it only in heaven. What you can and should
do during the time you use for occupations other than prayer
alone is to keep the thought of me as actively before your
mind as you can and the nature of your work permits, lifting
up the eyes of your soul toward me as often and as lovingly
as possible. Then you will be praying to me as ceaselessly
and continually as it is possible for poor mortals to do.

"As you will see, prayer is primarily thinking of me with
love — the more anyone loves me, the more he prays. Prayer
is the attention of the soul lovingly fixed on me. The more
loving that attention is, the better is the prayer."
                    — Retreat at Nazareth, November 1897, SA 74–75

To a Trappist (1898)

Your business now is to live alone with God and to be, until
your ordination, as though you and God were alone in the
universe. One must cross the desert and dwell in it to receive
the grace of God. It is here one drives out everything that is

not God. The soul needs to enter into this silence, this recollection, this forgetfulness of all created things by which God establishes his rule in it and forms within it the life of the spirit, the life of intimacy with God, the conversation of the soul with God in faith, hope, and charity. Later the soul will bring forth fruit exactly in the measure in which the inner life is developed in it. If there is no inner life, however great may be the zeal, the high intention, the hard work, no fruit will come forth; it is like a spring that would give out sanctity to others but cannot, having none to give; one can only give that which one has. It is in solitude, in that lonely life alone with God, in profound recollection of soul, in forgetfulness of all created things, that God gives himself to the soul that thus gives itself whole and entire to him.   — MH 139

•

I must consider God. I, a worm, am to lift my eyes to you, the Infinite. How is this possible? And yet it is possible, for you tell us that it is a duty. We alone, of all created things, can and should raise our hearts to you; rising through material beauty to the beauty of the soul and of spiritual things. Rising step by step upon the ladder of created things we can attain to the perception of the perfect Mind, adding perfections, eliminating imperfections, and carrying the thought of perfect beauty on to that excelling perfection, till we finally attain to the idea of what you are, my Father, my Creator, my Father, my Beloved; you who are there, a few feet from me, under the appearance of the Host, you are the Supreme Beauty. All created beauty, all beauty of Nature, the beauty of the sunset, of the sea lying like a mirror beneath the blue sky, of the dark forest, of the garden of flowers, of the mountains and the great spaces of the desert, of the snow and the ice, the beauty of a rare soul reflected in a beautiful face, all these beauties are but the palest reflection of yours, my God. All that has ever charmed my eyes in this world is but the poorest, the humblest reflection of your infinite Beauty.

O my God, give me the grace to see nothing else but you, nothing but you in all created things; never to be arrested by them, never to see the natural or spiritual beauty that is in them as being born of themselves, but only as being part of you.

Let my mind pierce through the veil and not rest on these poor things made of mingled life and nothingness, ruinous, decaying, empty. But, through all the Being that I see in created things, pass at once beyond their appearance and beyond their poor consistency and perceive the Essential Being to which all beings belong and which has cast a fragment of itself into these created things in which we take pleasure. If this fragment seems to us so lovely, how much more lovely is the perfect Being who has thrown it to us as alms, like a penny thrown to a beggar. My God, give me that Grace you gave to St. Teresa, never to attribute to created things themselves the spiritual or material beauty that may be in them, or to rest in them, for these come not from themselves, but from the Sovereign Being. To rest in them would be ungrateful, discourteous, an abuse of confidence, for God gave this beauty to created things that he may show himself to me, and my pleasure in them, to rouse my gratitude, through them, for his goodness, my love for his Beauty, and make me climb to his throne and there establish the life of my soul in adoration, in wondering contemplation and gratitude. So my conversation will be in heaven, since earthly sights can only let me guess at your beauty and your tender love.

And he is near me, this perfect Being, who is All Being, who is the only true Being, who is all Beauty, goodness, wisdom, love, knowledge, intelligence. Those creatures in whom

I admire a reflection of his perfection, on whom there falls a little ray of the infinite sunshine, are outside me, far removed from me, distant and separate, while you, who are Perfection, Beauty, Truth, Infinite and Essential Love, you are in me and around me. You fill me altogether... there is no particle of my body that you do not fill, and around me you are nearer than the air in which I move. How am I blessed! What happiness to be united so completely to Perfection itself; to live in it, to possess it living in myself! My God, you who are in me, in whom I am, let me know my happiness, and let me know my duty.

My God, give me a perpetual sense of your Presence, of your Presence in all around me, and at the same time that loving fear one feels in the presence of him one loves passionately, and which makes one, in the presence of one's Beloved, keep one's eyes upon him with great desire and firm purpose to do all that may please him and be for his good, and greatly fear to do or think anything that may displease or harm him.

In you, by you, and for you. Amen.

— Retreat at Nazareth, November 1897, MH 39–41

•

[*Jesus speaks:*] "Prayer is all intercourse of the soul with God. It is also the attitude of the soul when it contemplates God without words, solely occupied in contemplation, speaking its love with constant regard, though lips are silent and even thoughts are still. *The best prayer is the most loving prayer.* Prayer, in the widest sense of the word, may be either a silent contemplation or one accompanied by words. Words of adoration, love, self-immolation, the giving of all one's being, words of thanksgiving for the graces and blessings of God, for favors shown to oneself, or to others, words of regret in reparation for one's sins or those of others, words of supplication.

"*Praying,* you see, is above all to think of me with loving thoughts; and the more you love, the better you pray. Prayer is to have the attention lovingly fixed on me. The more loving the attention the better the prayer."

— Eight Days at Ephraim, 1898, MH 122–23

To a Poor Clare (1903)

In our prayers let us ask him to make us love him, and that mankind may love him; or perhaps the best thing of all is to say to him every morning that what we ask for ourselves we ask always for all men without exception. Then when we have said this we can leave others aside. We have done our very best for them. After this we need think no more of our fellow-creatures, but speak to the Spouse only of himself and ourselves as though we were alone in the world together. We can be *en tête à tête* with him speaking only of our love. Let us lose sight of all created things after having done our very best for them in our morning offering. The more we forget men, the more we can do for them; the more we ask the beloved Spouse, in close converse with him, and forgetting all else but him, to make us love him with all the power of our hearts, the greater good we can do for humanity which shares in all our petitions.   — MH 169

CONSOLATIONS

However sad I am when I kneel at the foot of the altar and say to Our Lord Jesus, "Lord, you are infinitely happy and lack nothing," I cannot help adding: I'm happy, too, and I lack nothing. Your happiness is enough for me.... This is true, it must be like that if we love our Lord.

—Easter 1891, SP 35

•

I do not ask Jesus for consolations (primarily because I do not deserve them), because if he granted them it would be such joy to hear him, to feel him deep in my heart, that I should be in paradise, and we cannot have our paradise both in this world and in the next. I ask only one thing of him: that I may be loyal to him. But alas, my loyalty is so weak.

It is right that a soul so lacking in fervor should never taste bliss. God sometimes allows us to be in such profound darkness that not a single star shines in our skies. The reason is that we must be reminded that we are on earth only to suffer, while following our gentle Savior along a dark and thorny path. We are pilgrims and strangers on earth. Pilgrims sleep in tents and sometimes forget everything else. Yes, on earth we are indeed in an alien world — we ought to hang up our harps and weep (Ps. 136:1–2).

In absolutely every situation my only desire is to fulfill the divine will. But alas, I have so little love for Jesus that I dare not call him my Beloved. Yet I want — I long — to love him more than anything on earth or in heaven. My heart and my life are his alone.

When you feel tired, sad, lonely, a prey to suffering, withdraw into the intimate sanctuary of your soul, and there you will find your *brother*, your *friend Jesus*, who will be your consolation, your stay and your strength.

[*Jesus speaks, answering him:*] "Putting it all in a single phrase, my child: abandon everything, and you will find all things." —Nazareth, 1897, SA 50–51

Meditation on Psalm 1

You tell me I shall be happy, filled with the happiness of true blessedness, on the last day — that even in my present wretchedness, I am a palm tree planted beside living waters, the living waters of God's will, love, and grace — and that I shall bring forth fruit in its proper season. You take the trouble to console me; I feel I am without fruit, without good works. I tell myself: it is eleven years since I was converted, and what have I done? What are my good works beside those of the saints? I see myself with hands empty of anything good. You take the trouble to console me, saying: You will bear in *your* proper season. But what season is that? The proper season for us all is the day of judgment. You promise that poor as I am if I persevere in the good fight with a good will I shall bear fruit at that last hour.

And you add: you will be a fine tree with leaves eternally green, and all your works will prosper in the end; they will all bear fruit in eternity. O God, how good you are! How divinely consoling is the Heart of Jesus! It is as though you had dictated these first words in the Book of Psalms to tell us what you once said by the Sea of Galilee: "My yoke is sweet and my burden light." I thank you, my God, for the consolation you give us, consolation of which our hearts stand in such great need.

—Meditations on the Psalms, 1898, SA 53

To His Sister

November 19, 1898

If we love Jesus we live much more in him than in ourselves. We forget our concerns so as to think only of what concerns him, and since he is in peace and ineffable blessedness, seated at the right hand of the Father, we participate, according to the measure of our love, in the peace and beatitude of our divine Beloved.

You ask me to pray for peace for you, my dear; the secret of peace is to love, love, love.   —SA 139–40

•

Everything that happens to me — it is the foundation of my soul — brings me always the same two things, sings to me the same two songs, the same two anthems, if I dare to say: the first is Joy, for in everything there is some glory for Jesus, something which glorifies his name, something which helps communion with him. . . . The second is: *Sanctify yourself, convert yourself! Conversion!* Everything tells me to convert myself, everything sings out to me of the necessity of sanctifying myself. Everything repeats to me and cries to me that, if good which I wish does not materialize, the fault lies within me and I must hasten to convert myself.

—September 30, 1902, Witness 103

•

A deep peace floods the soul, transitory things are nothing. We are walking toward God, contemplating his immense happiness and rejoicing forever in the thought of the infinite, perfect, unchangeable happiness of this God we love; we are happy with the happiness of the Beloved, and the thought of his unchangeable peace calms the soul. . . . The sight of my own nothingness does not weigh me down: it helps me forget myself and think only of him who is all in all.

—November 5, 1902, SP 37

To His Sister

Béni-Abbès, April 15, 1903

Alleluia! Life is like that; all joy, even good and holy joy, passes, except that which has its source in God alone, and in his own infinite joy; and even this may sometimes be hidden by divine permission from the most faithful hearts. It is only in heaven that joy will be unfailing, and rejoicing, unchanging, and perpetual. Let us join as far as we can here in the unchanging life of heaven. The dedicated can and ought to do so. Faith teaches us here what we shall there see clearly with our own eyes, and in the measure of our faith and our love we should be able to enjoy the immense glory of Jesus which is the joy of the Saints. Let us often remember that our Beloved is happy, and thank him for it with all our hearts.

Though we may suffer, our beloved Jesus is happy, that is enough for us, for it is him and not ourselves that we love. Though we are wretched sinners our Beloved is infinitely perfect and holy and glorious; that is enough, for it is him, not ourselves, that we love.

Though those that we love here on earth (and we are bound to love all human beings as brothers) may suffer or sin, still our Beloved is happy and glorious in the highest heaven; this should suffice, for it is him that we love "with all our hearts and with all our soul, with all our mind, and all our strength, and above all things."

Let us give him thanks unceasingly for his great Glory, as the Church does at the *Gloria in Excelsis* in the Mass. Let us join, even in this life, in the chorus of Saints and Angels in heaven, and cry with them, Holy, Holy, Alleluia.

—MH 170–71

To His Sister

April 1903

Sorrows and joys, consolation and trial, all come to you from the Sacred Heart, all is given by him for your very great good and your sanctification, and to increase your conformity to his will and your union to him. "All is good to those that love God." Hide yourself in the Heart of Jesus; he is our refuge, our shelter, the house of the swallow, the nest of the turtledove, the bark of Peter to carry us over the stormy waters. He is happy now. He has no more suffering to bear. When you are in sorrow think of his happiness and tell yourself that it is his happiness that you desire and not your own, him that you love, and not yourself, and beneath all your suffering and sadness, and your anxieties and worries you will be able to rejoice in his joy and feel his immense peace. Let the thought of the peace he enjoys in the "blessed and ever tranquil Trinity" fill you in this world with happiness and peace while you wait for the vision in the next which will give you peace and joy forever. — MH 171

•

It is only by looking out beyond this world, where everything passes away and dies, that we can know the true joy of hope in another life, to which this is only the prelude: a life where the good done here below will have its reward, and where the thirst of our spirits and hearts for light, truth, and love will be fully and eternally satisfied.

I am happy, very happy, in this hope and in faith in the truths God has revealed to us — truths beautiful as a poem, as the most beautiful of poems, for there are no poems in the world as beautiful as a simple treatise on dogmatic theology, the poem of divine love, on a different plane of wonder and beauty from the bare poems of our earthly loves. In this faith and hope, in the contemplation of this beauty and the fulfillment of the law of charity, the foundation of all Christian morality, "love all human beings as God loves them," my days flow by in a profound peace.

—December 15, 1905, SA 169–70

•

I love this desert; it is so good and wholesome to be alone, face to face with eternal things — truth washes over you like a flood. I find it hard to have to go on my travels and leave this solitude and silence; but the will of the Beloved, whatever it may be, must be not only preferred but loved, cherished, and blessed without measure: it must be loved as the Beloved himself is loved and as he loves, without measure.   —July 15, 1906, Memories 104

To Louis Massignon

July 15, 1916

Love consists not in feeling that we love, but in wanting to love. We love above all things what we want to love above all things. If it comes about that we do succumb to a temptation, it is because our love is too weak, not because it does not exist. Like St. Peter, we should weep, like him we should repent and humble ourselves — but also like him, we should say three times: "I love you. I love you. You know that despite my weakness and sins, I love you."

As for Jesus' love for us, he has proved it to us clearly enough for us to believe in it without being able to feel it. To feel we loved him and he loved us would be heaven. But heaven is not, except at rare moments and in rare cases, for us here below.   —SA 212

SUFFERING

It was at the moment when Jacob was on the road, poor, alone, when he sank naked to the ground in the desert to rest after a long journey on foot, it was at the moment when he was in the painful situation of an isolated traveler in the middle of a long voyage in a strange and savage country, without shelter, that was the moment when he found, in his sad condition, that God had heaped incomparable favors upon him.   —December 1896, Witness 57

To a Trappist

Nazareth, September 30, 1897

All we are trying to do is be one with Jesus, to reproduce his life in our own, to proclaim his teaching from the rooftops in our thoughts, words, and actions, to let him rule and live in us. He comes into us so frequently in the Holy Eucharist — may he establish his kingdom within us! If he gives us joys, we should accept them gratefully: the Good Shepherd gives us such sweet grasses to strengthen us and make us fit to follow him later along dry pathways. If he gives us crosses, we should embrace them: *bona crux* [good cross]. To be given a cross is the best grace of all: it is to walk hand in hand with Jesus more closely than ever, to relieve him by carrying his cross for him, as Simon of Cyrene did. It is our Beloved's invitation to us to declare and prove our love for him. In torments of soul and bodily suffering, "Let us rejoice and be glad"; Jesus is calling us, telling us to tell him we love him, and to go on telling him as long as our suffering lasts.

Every cross, great or small, every discomfort even, is an appeal from our Beloved, asking us to declare our love and

go on doing so while the cross lasts. When we think of it like
this, could we not wish that our cross could last for ever?
It will last as long as Jesus wishes. However sweet it may
be, however greatly loved, we desire it only as long as it is
Jesus' will for us. Your will, not ours, Brother Jesus. As for
ourselves, we should think no more of ourselves than as if
we did not exist. We should think only of you, our beloved
Spouse. We want not what seems good to us, but what is
good to you. We ask nothing for ourselves; all we ask is your
glory. "Hallowed be thy name; thy kingdom come; thy will
be done" in your children, in all men. May these things be
done in us. May we give all possible glory to you throughout
our lives. May we do your will — may we give all possible
solace to your Heart. That is all we want and all we need.
We are here at your feet, do with us as you will — whatever
it may be, do it according to your will. We have no will,
no wish except to fulfill your will, to do what seems good
to you.   —SA 53

•

There will always be unhappiness in our lives, and it is right
that there should be: unhappiness for the sake of the love
we bear — and rightly bear — ourselves and all men, and for
the sake, too, of the love we bear Jesus and in memory of
his sufferings. Then there will be the unhappiness caused by
the longing we cannot but have for justice — that is, for the
glory of God — and the pain we are bound to undergo when
we see injustice, and God being insulted.

But right as these sufferings are, they should not last long
in our souls. They should be transitory. What should endure
and be *our normal state — the state to which we should constantly return — is joy in the glory of God,* joy at seeing that

Jesus is suffering no longer, and will suffer no more, but is in bliss forever at the right hand of God.

—Retreat at Nazareth, November 1897, SA 97

To His Sister

May 8, 1899

Bona Crux! Through the cross we are united to him, who was nailed on it, our heavenly spouse. Every instant of our lives must be accepted as a favor, with all that it brings of happiness and suffering. But we must accept the cross with more gratitude than anything else. Our crosses detach us from earth and therefore draw us closer to God.

—MH 142–43

•

Jesus saved the world by his cross; by the cross we must continue the work of redemption to the end of time, letting Jesus live in us and make up all that has still to be undergone by Christ. Without the cross there can be no union with the crucified Jesus, no union with Jesus the Savior.

—September 30, 1902, SP 48

The Detachment, the Renunciation of Jesus

"To him that would take your cloak give your coat also." If I love Jesus I shall be attached to him alone, to his words, his example, his will. If I wish to possess him, to obey him, to imitate him, to be one with him, lose myself in him by losing my own will in his, all these things cry aloud the need for detachment from everything that is not him. The desire to possess nothing but him cries out: detachment. His words cry out: detachment. His example cries out: detachment. His will cries: detachment. I must resolve to see, unceasingly, Jesus in myself, dwelling within me with his Father.

I must work with all my strength to sanctify myself. Mortification, mortification, penance, death. It is when one is suffering most that one is most sanctified oneself and most sanctifies others. "If the grain of seed dieth not it bringeth not forth. When I shall be raised from the earth I will draw all men after me."

It was not by his divine words, not by his miracles, not by his good works that Jesus saved the world; it was by his cross.

The most fruitful hour of his life was that of his greatest abasement and annihilation, that in which he was plunged in suffering and humiliation.

—Notes on Retreat, 1904, MH 164–65

To His Cousin Marie on the Day of His Death

Our annihilation is the most powerful means we have to unite ourselves to Jesus and to save souls; that is what St. John of the Cross repeated in nearly every line. When one wishes to suffer and to love, one can. One does the most of what one tries the most to do. One feels that one suffers but one doesn't always feel that one loves, and that is added suffering. But one knows that one wishes to love, and wishing to love is to love. One finds that one doesn't love enough. That's true. One will never love enough. But Almighty God who knows of what he has molded us and who loves us more than a mother loves her child has told us — and he does not lie — that he will not cast out those who come to him.

—December 1, 1916, Witness 273

Epilogue

Final Witness

To *follow Jesus crucified, I must lead the life of the cross.*   —Nazareth, April 26, 1897

*With every passing year there grew in Foucauld the convic-
tion that he would die as a martyr. Perhaps, in light of the
vulnerability of his isolated existence, this required no special
prescience. Nevertheless the consciousness of violent death
and his readiness to meet this fate formed a part of Foucauld's spiritual discipline from quite early in his journey.
In part this was a feature of his identification with Jesus,
who died on the cross: the servant should expect no better
than his master. But it also reflected his deep embrace of the
paschal mystery: "Unless the grain of wheat falls into the
ground and dies it bears no fruit." The end for Charles de
Foucauld — in circumstances remarkably close to those he
had envisioned — came on December 1, 1916.*

•

[*Jesus speaks:*] "Your thought of death: Think that you
may die a martyr, despoiled of everything, stretched on
the ground, covered with blood and wounds, violently and
painfully killed. Wish this to happen today. If I am to give

121

you this infinite grace, be faithful in watching and in carrying the cross. Consider that such a death should be the object of your whole life; see in it how little other things matter. Think often of this death so as to be ready for it and to judge things at their true value in the light of it."

—Nazareth, 1897, MH 131

•

Now I should like to ask something of you myself: pray that I may love; pray that I may love Jesus; pray that I may love his cross; pray that I may love the cross, not for its own sake, but as the only means, the only way of giving glory to Jesus: "The grain of wheat does not bring forth fruit unless it dies.... And I, if I be lifted up ... will draw all things to myself." As St. John of the Cross points out, it was at the moment of his supreme abasement, the hour of his death, that Jesus did the most good, that he saved the world. So then ask Jesus that I may truly love the cross, for it is indispensable if we are going to do good to souls. And I carry it very little, I am cowardly. Virtues are ascribed to me which I do not possess — and I am the most fortunate of men. So pray for my conversion, that I may love Jesus and do at all times what would be most pleasing to him. Amen.

—February 27, 1903, SA 151

From the Rule of the Little Brothers of the Sacred Heart

The Little Brothers are to remember each day that one of the favors their Spouse Jesus has lavished on them is the possibility, the firm hope, of ending their life by martyrdom: let them prepare themselves for this happy end: let them behave at each moment as befits souls called by the Spouse's goodness to receive — perhaps soon — this infinite favor.... Their desires and prayers should plead for the blessed moment when they can give their Beloved this greatest sign of their love; they must be always worthy of such a great vocation.... And when the moment comes, let them, without a shadow of defense (we are forbidden to possess, carry, or use weapons), "like sheep among wolves," as meek as the divine Lamb, humble, overflowing with gratitude, praying for their persecutors, letting Jesus make up in their deaths all that he has still to undergo, offering themselves to him for his greater glory, for all the intentions for which he offered himself on Calvary, uniting the sacrifice of their lives with the sacrifice of his life, in peace, blessing, and love, letting him live and act in them more than ever at this supreme, blessed hour, called as they are to imitate him in his death as in his life, shed their blood and exhale their souls in Jesus, by Jesus, like Jesus, for Jesus! —SP 86–87

Stray Notes for Meditation, 1916

[*Jesus speaks:*] *Watch and Pray.* "I invite you to spend the night in converse with me. Will you refuse?

"I ask you to stay awake to contemplate me, to tell me that you love me — to adore me: to pray for all men: to ask pardon of me for those who are sinning at this moment, and who stay awake for the purpose of sinning."

If I neglect to stay awake and am too lazy to rise, (1) I am refusing to lay myself at the feet of Our Lord, and keep him company, we two together, when he is calling me to do so. (2) I am preferring to sleep rather than to be alone with Our Lord, in intimate converse and union with him, the Spouse of my soul. (3) I am making a bad preparation for martyrdom. "They answered him nothing." They did not know what to say to their friend Jesus. "They who in proud courage aspired to martyrdom are dumb: and soon will fly in confusion."

Mortification. Through my cowardice over mortifying myself I am refusing to carry the cross. I am refusing to be a victim with Our Lord. I am refusing to follow him since he has said "Veni." I am refusing to help him carry the cross with Simon of Cyrene. While he falls beneath the weight of the cross for me, and because of me, I refuse to touch it with the tip of my finger. I see him suffer and I let him suffer alone, I do not wish to suffer with him. I leave that to others and abandon him myself. I am resisting his invitation to my inner self, asking me to show him some sign of my love. I am refusing to obey his orders, I who have so often told him that to obey him was my greatest joy. I do not love him enough to put myself out for him. I know that all suffering, all trouble that I take upon myself is a sign of love given to him: but I prefer to enjoy my ease to giving it up to him. For me, and because of me, he suffered cold, hunger, thirst, fatigue, labors, his Agony and the Passion; and I seek to leave him alone to suffer and to spare myself all discomfort, all suffering of body or soul. He holds out his hand to me to walk with me, hand in hand, through life; I let go his hand and let him go his way alone, and I on my side seek a less arduous way. He asks me to make him an oblation, a sacrifice, and I refuse.

Love My Life in God. The most perfect way. I should carry on in myself the life of Jesus: think his thoughts, repeat his words, his actions. May it be he that lives in me. I must be the image of Our Lord in his hidden life: I must proclaim, by my life, the Gospel from the rooftops. *Veni.* My courage must be equal to my will. "Seek thyself in me. Seek me in thyself." "It is time to love God." Seek God only. Kindness. Gentleness. Sweetness. Courage. Humility. —MH 184–86

My Future on Earth, My Death, Judgment, Heaven or Hell

Pardon and *Misericordias Domini in aeternum cantabo.* Such are my past and my present. What is to be my future? Is it to be long or short on earth? Happy or sorrowful? Holy as I long for it to be, or full of sin? From which I implore you to save me. No one can know. It will be as you will it, my God. I only ask that it may not be spent in offending you. That cannot be your will. You have commanded us all to be perfect, and you have loaded me with graces and said, "To him that hath much more shall be given." So whatever may be my future, whether long or a day's span, happy or sorrowful, it must be your will that it be sanctified. What shall I do that it may be so?

"This life will be followed by death. You wish for a martyr's death. You know how cowardly you are, but you know too that you can do all things in him who gives strength, that I am All Powerful in my creatures. Ask night and day for it, but always with this condition, that it be my will, and for my glory and my pleasure which I know you desire and pray for above all things. And have confidence; I will grant what you ask, that which is for my greater glory. It is good to ask for this, for 'there is no greater love than to give your life for the beloved,' and it is right to wish to give me this 'greatest love of all.' "   — Retreat at Nazareth, MH 66–67